CONNECT

S

Usi
Make

Stev

Published by:
Empowered Life Publishing
Lawrence, NY

Disclaimer: This book is not intended to offer medical or mental health advice. If you have any questions regarding the appropriateness of any of the exercises described herein, consult your healthcare provider.

Cover & interior design by The Book Couple
www.thebookcouple.com

Printed in the United States of America.

To my children,
Eric, Jonny, and Briana—
For your love and support,
and for keeping me real

CONTENTS

ACKNOWLEDGMENTS

I want to thank the team that worked with me on this new and revised edition, which was originally published in 2010 as *Connect for Success: The Ultimate Guide to Workplace Relationships.* This book is now the first volume of the Empowered Life Series and will be followed next by an updated edition of *Handbook for Early Career Success.*

Like most remodeling projects, this revision was a lot more involved and demanding than I ever could have anticipated. But neither could I have anticipated just how creative, professional, and invaluable my new editorial and design partners, Carol and Gary Rosenberg (aka The Book Couple), would be. Thanks, guys. And I was very lucky to have Hannah Poster (aka my gifted and talented niece) to edit and fine tune. She doesn't miss a thing.

Without the incredible generosity and talent of my friends, family, and professional colleagues, *Connect for Success* would never have left the ground. I am so appreciative of their time and contributions and wish to formally and publicly thank them.

My experience participating in one of Nancy Petaja's workshops more than ten years ago left a powerful impression and helped shape both the content and approach of *Connect for Success.* I am especially appreciative of the sections she helped develop: Levels of Listening and the Career Entry Checklist. Shelley Byan's development of many of the Connect for Success Workshop exercises contributed significantly to the straightforward, practical, and engaging quality of the book. Beth Mead is a gifted business writer who was also on my team from the beginning. She deserves much credit for making even the most complex ideas accessible.

Through this process I discovered that there are those special individuals who, no matter how busy they are, find the time to help. Thank you, thank you, thank you to Bob DeFillippo, Linda Revaz, Danella Schiffer, JoAnn Ryan, Carol Binen, Cathy Bergstrom, Terry Miller, Lori McDonough, Lisa Paik, Roy Schwartz, Paula Schwartz, Jackie Nash, Barbara Lurie, Dene Vitale, Colette Gambino, Barbara Lynne Boslow, and Rich Rassmann.

I want to acknowledge David Merrill and Roger Reid, Robert and Dorothy Bolton, and Gordon Thomas for the exceptional personality-style models they honed and from which the Connecting Styles Survey and Model evolved.

I am deeply appreciative of the generous guidance and friendship of Bernie Kessler and Ed Betof, both role models as organizational psychologists. Ed's book *Just Promoted: How to Survive and Thrive in Your First 12 Months as a Manager* (McGraw-Hill, 1992), written with Fredric Harwood, helped shape some of the ideas found in "Entry: Connecting to the Organization (Chapter 18)" in this book.

I want to thank the three mentors most influential in my professional development: Bob Nelson, originally my client and now my West Coast partner, who may be the most naturally helpful coach and teacher with whom I have ever been involved; Ray Knight, my Brandeis University psychology professor, who taught me how to think like a psychologist (as in behavioral scientist); and Larry Epstein, my mentor and supervisor whose deep understanding of how people grow, succeed, and find happiness serve as core principles upon which *Connect for Success* is based.

Finally, I want to thank Nancy Borghesi, who can always sense where I am trying to go and provide the counsel, encouragement, and inexhaustible support to get me there.

INTRODUCTION

Over the past twenty-five years I have had the good fortune to coach hundreds of individuals representing a wide cross section of industries—some whose careers were extremely successful and some who, despite their abundant talent, found themselves sidelined and frustrated. Without exception, the most important factor determining long-term success and satisfaction was the quality of the relationships each of these individuals formed with the people around them.

While most followed the "Golden Rule"—treat others as *you* would like to be treated—to guide their behavior, we found that those who connected most effectively across the widest range of personalities treated others as *they* (others) would like to be treated. *Connect for Success* provides the relationship-building insights and tools that will enable you to do just that: to interact with an understanding and respect for who *you* are and who *they* are. You will be able to apply our proven, common sense approach to forming strong connections with people you meet for the first time, making good relationships better, and improving long-standing difficult relationships that directly or indirectly limit your success and wear on your nerves.

Unfortunately, strong connections and solid working relationships with colleagues seem to be few and far between. If you ran an electric current through the communication lines that connect all employees in most workgroups, it would barely light up a bulb. And yet people seem to accept or ignore ongoing interpersonal conflict, writing if off as "office politics." Why? After all, if a company's financial resources were wasted at the rate trust and honest communication between people seem to be, the contributing problems would be identified and addressed immediately.

The relationship between Michael and Jane, long-term colleagues who should be working collaboratively but instead avoid each other, illustrates some of the reasons why conflict due to misconnection is rarely addressed:

Blaming the other person: Most people attribute misconnections to the behavior and habits of the other person, while seeing themselves as victims who are simply trying to do what's right.

Michael: "Jane is constantly in the details. She analyzes everything to death and never wants to make a decision. Everything has to be perfect. She never tells you what she really feels."

Jane: "Michael just can't stay focused. He is constantly going off on tangents and wasting valuable time with ideas that are totally unrealistic and then doesn't let anybody else talk."

Taking it personally: Michael and Jane read negative intentions into each other's behavior, turning the conflict from misconnect to personal affront, and thereby hardening the standoff.

Michael: "Jane is afraid of change. She is totally passive-aggressive. She's a control freak."

Jane: "Michael is so self-centered and immature."

In reality, they both experience themselves as doing what they do out of good intentions. It's just that both truly believe their approach is superior to that of the other, and each can point to several people who would agree (people just like them). From Jane's perspective, her behavior is driven by the desire to protect the organization from sloppy and impulsive decisions. Unnecessary uncertainty and confusion are hot buttons that increase her anxiety and lead to an even greater attention to detail. Expressing her feelings or opinions when she is unsure of what is occurring would just make her more anxious.

As Michael sees it, his behavior furthers innovation and excellence and protects against the bureaucracy and "analysis-paralysis" caused by overanalytical perfectionists like Jane. He also sees himself as helping Jane to loosen up and express her feelings more openly and directly—behavior that he deems to be "healthier" than holding things in—a judgment that she resents. The more remote Jane becomes, the more rejected Michael (who takes things very personally) feels, which in turn leads him to push even harder for recognition and acceptance in ways that irritate and alienate Jane even more—*allowing frustration to totally dominate their impressions of each other and obscure the value they each add.*

We can expect the Michael and Jane standoff to last indefinitely, side by side with countless misconnects that exist in organizations (and families)—misconnects that form like plaque on the vital arteries through which a full range of diverse ideas and perspectives must flow to get the full benefit of the collective IQ of the workgroup. In other words, everyone loses, including the organization.

Connect for Success will enable you to identify and address misconnects directly and constructively before they become personal. What drives personal and counterproductive conflicts like Michael and Jane's is lack of awareness of one's own Connecting Style and its impact on others. *Connect for Success* will sharpen your self-awareness and provide tools and advice that will give you control over the quality of your relationships along with the ability to self-direct your own path to more trusting and enduring connections.

The Layout of *Connect for Success*

Part One introduces the "Six Basic Connecting Needs" (Chapter 1) and lays out the specific behaviors that will make the difference between engaging openness and cooperation versus defensiveness and competition.

No matter how well you know the behavioral rules for connecting, if you don't know how you come across or understand your

"Blind Spot" (Chapter 2), you cannot effectively influence how others will react to you.

Part Two, "Connecting Style" (Chapters 3–11), provides a much clearer and more realistic sense of who you are as others see you. By following the directions for the easily self-administered Connecting Styles Survey, you will find out which of four connecting styles best describes you. This section equips you with a wealth of information about all four styles and provides invaluable insights about yourself and others, including who you are as others see you, the situations that bring out the best in you, the team roles to which you gravitate, and your blind spots. In addition to the self-awareness rules and tools you can apply to nearly every aspect of your life, the Connecting Style Model will help you to discover a very specific and direct path to optimal effectiveness. In order to get the full benefit of the book, it is essential that you complete the Connecting Style Survey in the book or online at myconnecting style.com before proceeding to the sections that follow it.

"Connecting Across Styles" and "Guidelines for Connecting with Each Style" (Chapters 7 and 8) provide guidance for building relationships with the 75 percent of the world whose styles are different from yours.

"Increasing Role Versatility" (Chapter 9) takes you through an exercise to sharpen your awareness of the roles in which you feel least comfortable and will help you develop a strategy to make you more effective in those roles.

Chapter 10, "Connecting from Your Sweet Spot," teaches you how to apply your Connecting Style awareness to engage and influence others with maximum intended impact *without changing who you are!*

Chapter 11 provides specific instructions for "Assessing Connecting Style in Others" and an exercise to test your Connecting Style assessment skills.

Part Three introduces you to the skills and habits most critical to workplace relationship building. "Listening" (Chapter 12) is the most powerful, yet underdeveloped, means of connecting across all styles. "Self-Discipline" (Chapter 13) and "Habit Change" (Chapter 14) are the competencies most critical to developing and mastering the skills and behaviors you will be learning as you read this book.

In the highly networked global workplace where career mobility is essential to a successful career, "Networking" (as described in Chapter 15) has become a requirement. This chapter helps you to apply your Connecting Style awareness to become a more effective and happier networker.

"Stress Resilience" (Chapter 16) provides insights and advice for dealing with stress. You can take the Stress Resilience Survey to find out more about how effectively you are currently managing it and to learn what you can do to increase your resilience.

Part Four, "Connecting at Work," provides insight into the subtle but powerful influences that diverse personalities and cultures exert and describes techniques for harnessing those dynamics to survive and thrive. Chapter 17, "Styles at Work," illustrates how the Six Basic Connecting Needs and Connecting Style awareness can be applied to significantly enhance interpersonal effectiveness at work. Chapter 18, "Entry: Connecting to the Organization," helps you to apply the *Connect for Success* principles to successfully transition from "outsider" to "trusted member" of the organization.

Chapter 19, "Leveraging Connecting Style Diversity," teaches you how to apply the *Connect for Success* principles to build teams and organizations with the style diversity that leads to stronger problem solving, innovation, and overall performance when facing challenges.

Chapter 20, "Staying Grounded," helps prepare you for the challenge of assimilating to organizational culture, competitive pressure, and politics without losing sight of who you are, what you stand for, and why you are there.

Finally, for those of you who are helping your teens to transition into the workplace at the same time as you are working on making the most of your career, I applied the Connect for Success relationship-building principles to "Preparing Our Teens for Career Success" (Appendix A).

Exercises can be found throughout the book immediately following this symbol:

These exercises are designed to help you connect information, insights, and advice to your own personal experience and development.

Appendix B contains "Development Planning Forms" you can use to translate your self-awareness into specific, actionable plans that will facilitate genuine and enduring behavior change, which will result in more effective relationship-building.

Appendix C, "On-Boarding Checklist," provides a tracking tool that lists the key tasks and activties discussed in Chapter 18, "Entry: Connecting to the Organization."

I'm very glad to be sharing this book with you and hope that it benefits you in ways intended and totally unintended. The fact is, everybody gets something different from *Connect for Success*, and the more I can tap into the readers' experiences and incorporate them into subsequent editions, the better. But none of it is possible unless I hear back from you. Please e-mail feedback, experiences, questions, or suggestions to me at steve@stevenluriephd.com.

The road to more satisfying and successful relationships begins here. Good luck, and enjoy the journey!

PART ONE

Connecting for Success

CHAPTER 1

SIX BASIC CONNECTING NEEDS

*"And, in the end, the love you take
is equal to the love you make."*
—Paul McCartney, "The End," *Abbey Road*

How do I connect with others (coworkers, customers, patients, clients, supervisors, subordinates, senior executives) in a way that leads them . . .

- to be comfortable working with me?
- to trust in and rely upon me?
- to be open to my ideas?
- to include me in important decisions?
- to give me the benefit of the doubt?
- to choose me for key roles and jobs?

How do I keep others from . . .

- being resistant or defensive?
- discounting or dismissing my contribution?
- misunderstanding my good intentions?

How receptive or defensive other people are toward you is based largely upon:

- Your ability to communicate in the style most comfortable for the receiver. We call this *Connecting Style* and will address this in detail in the next section.

- The extent to which your behavior supports or frustrates the following *Six Basic Connecting Needs* in the people with whom you are interacting. These are the need to feel:

  1. Basic trust

  2. Understood

  3. Respected

  4. Empowered

  5. Valued

  6. Included

When your behavior supports these needs in others, you will create a receptive and supportive audience. Conversely, violation of one or more of these needs leads to defensive or antagonistic reactions. Once you identify the specific need or needs that have been frustrated, you can take action to support them and rebuild trust. A description of these six needs follows. Although each need is different, you will notice that they overlap one another. Pay close attention to the behaviors that support or frustrate each need.

SUPPORTING THE SIX BASIC CONNECTING NEEDS

The other person needs to feel:	You support their need by:	You frustrate their need by:
BASIC TRUST I trust that you are who you say you are. I don't have to watch my back. Your behavior reflects integrity, candor, and high moral and ethical standards. I feel secure in knowing that you are sincere, well intentioned, and have my best interests at heart.	❏ Being sincere and genuine ❏ Keeping confidential discussions confidential ❏ Being dependable; delivering on promises; following up on commitments; being on time ❏ Showing you have the courage of your convictions, and standing up for your beliefs, even if they are unpopular ❏ Taking responsibility for mistakes ❏ Demonstrating loyalty ❏ Expressing disagreements directly rather than being a "yes" person	❏ Having hidden agendas ❏ Telling half-truths or embellishing ❏ Sharing confidential information or taking part in gossip ❏ Covering up mistakes ❏ Blaming others ❏ Taking credit for other's work ❏ "Working the system" or taking inappropriate advantage of policy
UNDERSTOOD You get me! You understand what I am saying, how I feel about it, and what it means to me.	❏ Listening ❏ Demonstrating interest in learning what it is like to be in the other person's shoes ❏ Restating what you hear ❏ Asking good questions	❏ Assuming you already understand ❏ Seeking to be understood before demonstrating that you understand ❏ Prematurely prescribing solutions ❏ Arguing or disagreeing without fully understanding ❏ Using body language that says you aren't listening

The other person needs to feel:	You support their need by:	You frustrate their need by:
RESPECTED I am treated in a way that acknowledges and recognizes my status, experience, knowledge, domain, authority, values, customs, and preferences, whether I am a mailroom clerk or CEO!	❏ Demonstrating that you have paid close attention to what is important to the other person ❏ Listening ❏ Apologizing once you realize you have "stepped on someone's toes" ❏ Taking other people's needs seriously, but not taking yourself seriously—modesty and self-deprecating humor go a long way ❏ Understanding how other people see their roles, priorities, and hot-button issues ❏ Recognizing the sacrifices, efforts, and accomplishments of others ❏ Demonstrating appreciation ❏ Supporting other people's position, power, and status as they define it ❏ Working through traditional channels and chain of command ❏ Asking for help, expertise, and consultation	❏ Not taking the time to understand what is important to others ❏ Being sarcastic or using humor to put others down ❏ Condescending, critical, or dismissive behavior ❏ Violating role boundaries, chain of command, or tradition ❏ Inflating your contribution and minimizing or ignoring the contribution made by others ❏ Coming across as a missionary on a quest to civilize and convert ("Let me tell you how we did it at ABC Company . . ."), rather than as an anthropologist trying to learn and understand
EMPOWERED You respect my autonomy. I feel free to make my own decisions and not be micromanaged or controlled. I feel I run my own life. I have ownership for my work and its outcome and full accountability for the results.	❏ Asking for permission to enter others' space: "Do you mind if I ask a question . . . make a suggestion . . . interrupt for a moment . . . give you some feedback?" ❏ Allowing others to figure things out for themselves and arrive at their own solutions ❏ Giving choices ❏ Using a participative leadership style	❏ Forcing unwanted opinions or advice on others ❏ Telling others what to do ❏ Keeping others out of the decision-making loop ❏ "Rescuing" others when they haven't asked for your help

The other person needs to feel:	You support their need by:	You frustrate their need by:
VALUED I am appreciated for what I do and who I am. I am perceived as making a difference, adding value, and contributing to something important.	❑ Finding merit in what others say and do ❑ Thanking people in person or through "thank you" notes or voicemail messages ❑ Expressing appreciation for how you or others have benefited from something the other person said or did ❑ Asking for advice or help	❑ Criticizing ❑ One-upping ❑ Discounting or dismissing ❑ Prescribing solutions or solving other's problem directly before they ask ❑ Boasting
INCLUDED I belong. I am invited into the inner circle. I feel like a vital part of the community or team.	❑ Asking other's opinion ❑ Consulting with others ❑ Asking others to join committees ❑ Using others as a sounding board ❑ Sharing something personal ❑ Inviting others (to meetings, lunch, etc.)	❑ Excluding others ❑ Making decisions without input from others ❑ Keeping to yourself ❑ Having sidebar conversations in group gatherings

Notice that some behaviors, like "listening" and "finding merit," support almost all of these universal needs. It's no wonder that these behaviors are the everyday habits of effective relationship builders. These include:

- Behaving with modesty and humility.

- Treating people with respect, acceptance, and never talking down to them.

- Being polite.

- Listening, listening, listening, and demonstrating that you understand more than just the message but also its context and the emotions behind it, too.

- Communicating in a fashion that takes into account the listener's communication style.

- Taking the time to understand and show respect for the needs, preferences, style, values, and accomplishments of the people with whom you work.

- Demonstrating appreciation by finding merit: giving credit, skillful praise, and thanks for good work and avoiding criticism.

- Going out of your way to be supportive (and keeping critical feelings about others to yourself).

- Including others by getting their advice and sharing your ideas, opinions, and feelings.

- Following up on promises.

- Being sincere.

- Accepting responsibility for your own mistakes and decisions.

- Apologizing when you have offended someone.

Remember, you get what you give!

1. Review all of the behaviors in the second and third columns of the table on pages 11–13, and in the box on the left of each item, place a checkmark next to any behavior that you believe you can improve in your day-to-day interactions.

2. Go back and select the three behaviors that you feel will be most important for you to address during the next few months.

3. Following the instructions on pages 175–176, create a development plan for each of those behaviors. Use the forms on pages 176–180.

CHAPTER 2

THE BLIND SPOT

*"They almost always report feeling blindsided when
they hit that ceiling and discover the gap between their
positive intentions and their actual negative impact
of their behavior on others."*

—BARBARA KOVACH[1]

Unfortunately, we're not always aware of when we are supporting or frustrating the Six Basic Connecting Needs. Most
often, it is the behaviors we are not aware of that have the greatest impact on how people feel about us. These include nonverbal
behaviors such as facial expression, tone of voice, or eye contact. In
other words, most of the things that people do to irritate others are
in a "blind spot."

Just as we are partially blind to the negative impact we can
have on others, most of us are largely unaware of what we do that
makes us valued and appreciated. I don't think I really understood
this until I was nearly fifteen years into my management-con-
sulting career, when the general counsel of a major entertainment
company asked me to lunch to discuss a serious personnel issue in
his department.

This very senior executive was not only an important client, but the organizational decisions he made had important consequences for many individuals across a number of entertainment divisions, and I was quite conscious of wanting to provide the best counsel possible. The restaurant he chose happened to be very crowded, and, with its very high ceilings, I found myself straining to hear as he told me the details of his challenge. I said, "Excuse me, would you please repeat that? I couldn't hear what you were saying." After about ten minutes of "Sorry," "Say again?" and "Pardon me," I resigned myself to the fact that we would have to continue the discussion after lunch or reschedule. As we were leaving the restaurant, I was about to suggest we reschedule when he turned to me to thank me for being so helpful. He was extremely appreciative of my consultation and felt very good about the solution that came out of our "discussion."

Good thing I couldn't hear well enough to analyze the issues and provide him sage advice. Through no fault of my own, I gave him what he really needed—the opportunity to talk through his problem with someone who was strenuously listening to his every word, while providing him the space to formulate his own solution. Through that accident, I became aware of how much I had been overrating the importance of advice-giving as the key to being helpful while I had been underrating the power of listening, especially when working with very self-reliant and competent people.

It's hard to know when we are overusing the behaviors that come most naturally to us. I recently sat in on a meeting, held by a rather forceful but well-meaning senior executive, intended to pump up and empower a new team he had inherited. The executive wanted to let his team know how important their feedback was to him and how open he was to hearing it. He spent about twenty minutes telling story after story about how feedback had helped him over the years, but he ran out of time before anyone else had the chance to speak. While he understood intellectually how important feedback from people is, his habit of holding one-way conversations contradicted that message and announced that his need to talk still outweighed his interest in listening to what others had to say.

Finally, a very nurturing but conflict-averse young employee was sharing how worried she was about what people at work would think of her after she finally insisted that two people who were constantly fooling around during meetings stop. She was concerned and said, "They are going to think I am a real bitch." The reality was that the other people at the meeting were so relieved to see her stand up for herself that they looked like they were ready to applaud.

These vignettes illustrate another important point about blind spots. Most of the time, the strengths we are least aware of are qualities that are typical of styles totally opposite from our own. More forcefully assertive people overestimate their value as drivers of results or solvers of problems, and they underestimate the power of listening and being supportive. More quietly assertive people underestimate the positive impact of forceful behavior.

Just as a car's blind spot is blamed for so many automobile crashes, so too is the human blind spot responsible for many of our career crashes. However, as we learned in driver's education, once you know about the blind spot you are responsible for doing the hard work of turning your head around to look before changing lanes or pulling out of your parking spot. Once you look where your mirror cannot see, it is no longer a blind spot. Thus, our behavioral blind spot will be trouble for us only to the extent that we don't bother to get feedback from others about how they see us or don't observe people's reactions to our behavior in the moment.

Understanding what is in your blind spot is a lifelong process, so why not start now?

The following chapters on Connecting Style will provide invaluable information about what may be hiding in your blind spot and the impact—both positive and negative—that these unintentional behaviors are likely to have on others.

1. Identify three people who know you well, but each in a different context, and ask each for feedback about your blind spot.

2. Prior to getting their feedback, write down what you think they might say.

   _____

   _____

   _____

3. Ask them to share with you what they think are your blind spots, including strengths and weaknesses. Make sure they know that this is an important part of your professional development and that you want to apply their feedback to improve your effectiveness. If they seem to be having trouble understanding what you are looking for, give them a copy of this chapter to read.

4. Write down their comments and refer to them after you have had the chance to complete the Connecting Style Survey in Chapter 4. How does your profile stack up against their descriptions of you?

   _____

   _____

   _____

   _____

   _____

   _____

PART TWO

Connecting Style

CHAPTER 3

INTRODUCING CONNECTING STYLE

"Human beings are the most social animal on our planet. Only three other animals (termites, eusocial insects, and naked mole rats) construct social networks as complex as ours, and we are the only one whose complex social networks include unrelated individuals."

—Elizabeth W. Dunn, Daniel T. Gilbert, and Timothy D. Wilson[2]

WHAT IS CONNECTING STYLE?

Connecting Style refers to the "signature" behavior pattern that characterizes the way a person interacts with the world. Style is so deeply engrained and instinctive that it's hardly noticeable to the person him- or herself—"Style? I'm just being me!" But to everybody else, Connecting Style is recognizable as "who someone is" and significantly impacts the impression the person makes on others.

And knowing into which style someone falls provides invaluable information about the best approach to building a strong connection with him or her. Connecting Style tells you about how someone is likely to approach relationships, communicate, solve problems, deal with conflict (or not), make decisions, partner, and lead others. Connecting Style even tells you the kinds of people an individual is likely to get along with best, as well as the habits and behaviors he or she is likely to find most irritating. So understanding someone's style allows you to tune into that person's needs, preferences, and reactions. Add to that an awareness of how that style interacts with your style, and you have a foundation for successful communication and relationship building in and out of the workplace.

HOW DID THE CONNECTING STYLE SURVEY COME ABOUT?

Starting in 1964 with the social styles personality model developed by David Merrill and Roger Reid,[3] at least one dozen four-style preference personality models have been developed and used extensively in various settings including schools, the workplace, and counseling centers each with its unique strengths and limitations. The Connecting Style model I developed takes what I believe are the best features of each of these models and integrates them with behavioral dimensions I discovered to be most relevant to success in today's world. My highest priority in developing the Connecting Style model was to make it as developmentally focused as possible. This means providing people with a path that could readily take them from "awareness" (of what was most natural and comfortable for them) to increasingly higher levels of effectiveness without changing the essence of who they are.

The result was the *Connecting Style Survey,* a simple yet powerful tool with a number of important advantages borne out by feedback collected from readers and workshop participants over the past several years:

1. Unlike other surveys, the Connecting Style Survey is quickly and easily self-administered and scored and quite accurate.

2. You can learn how to use behavioral observation to assess the Connecting Styles of others—even people you just met.

3. The Connecting Style model helps you predict and thereby pre-pare for the sudden and often counterproductive behavior changes brought on by stress.

4. The style descriptions, insights, and style-related recommenda-tions are nonthreatening and easily grasped, yet powerful and compelling. The insights are readily applied both inside and out-side of the workplace.

5. The insights gleaned from the Connecting Style Survey and tools are applicable to the development of individuals, workgroups, and organizations.

6. Connecting Style tools, tips, and principles can be readily applied to improve relationship-building, communications, influence, and leadership effectiveness.

7. The tool resonates powerfully with audiences ages fourteen to eighty, from people on the loading dock to those in corner offices.

Now let's introduce the two aspects of connecting that deter-mine one's Connecting Style. People fall into one of four Connect-ing Styles based on two aspects of their observable behavior: how they connect emotionally (emotional responsiveness) and how forcefully versus quietly they connect (assertiveness).

1. *Emotional responsiveness* refers to the degree to which a person responds to and expresses emotions in behaviorally observable ways. Some are less emotionally responsive or task-oriented and others are more emotionally responsive or relationship-oriented.

2. *Assertiveness* refers to how *quietly* or *forcefully* a person connects.

Before completing the *Connecting Style Survey Scoring Grid* form (page 28), review the behavioral qualities on the following page, which determine whether you would be considered more relation-ship- or task-oriented, and more quietly or forcefully assertive.

Task-Oriented	Relationship Oriented
1. Information focused (Pay attention to facts, data and the task at hand; when people react emotionally it makes me uncomfortable and is counterproductive to achieving the goal.)	1. People focused (Pay attention to people's feelings, concerns and motivations; when people react emotionally it helps me to understand the whole story.)
2. Less concerned with gaining approval and avoiding rejection	2. More concerned with gaining approval and avoiding rejection
3. Control feelings	3. Express feelings
4. Serious, formal, less approachable on a personal level	4. Warm, open, approachable on a personal level
5. Body language reveals limited range of emotions	5. Body language reveals wide range of feelings
6. Facial expression reveals limited range of emotions	6. Facial expression reveals wide range of feelings
7. Voice tone and variation reveal limited range of feelings	7. Voice tone and variation reveal wide range of feelings

Quietly Assertive	Forcefully Assertive
1. More quiet (More reserved and measured; keep a lot to myself; avoid the spotlight; don't like to force my ideas on a group.)	1. More forceful (More direct and certain; say what's on my mind; comfortable in the spotlight; urge others to accept my ideas.)
2. Listen / reflect (Conscious of not taking more than my share of time talking in a group; gather information and impressions and voice opinions once they are more clearly formulated.)	2. Talk / act (Have a lot to say and can take over a conversation if others let me; share my opinions even when others know more about the subject or topic.)
3. Move less and slower	3. Move more and faster
4. Talk softer and slower	4. Talk louder and faster
5. Lean back when making a point	5. Lean forward when making a point
6. Less confrontational (Pull back/ avoid when challenged or attacked.)	6. More confrontational (Push back/ confront when challenged or attacked.)
7. Decide more carefully	7. Decide more quickly

CHAPTER 4

SELF-SCORING THE CONNECTING STYLE SURVEY

Please refer to the Connecting Style Survey Self-Scoring Grid on page 28 as you read through the following instructions.

You can also take the Connecting Style Survey online at www.myconnectingstyle.com.

---

1. **First determine whether your style is more *task-oriented* or *relationship-oriented*, and to what extent.** Under "Task-Oriented" and "Relationship-Oriented" are seven pairs of behavioral descriptors. For each of the seven pairs, select the descriptor that best describes you by circling the number next to the item. For example, referring to the first pair in the illustration, Nancy perceives herself to be more naturally people-focused than information-focused, so she circled the number next to "People-Focused."

   The first question that comes up concerns how to respond when you act differently depending on where you are and with whom. For example, at work you see yourself as more information-focused but with your friends, more people-focused. If this is the case, choose the behavior that feels most natural or requires the least amount of energy and effort. If you are still unsure, choose the item that you believe the majority of people who know you best would describe you.

Nancy went on to circle the numbers next to all seven descriptors under "Relationship-Oriented." Nancy would be considered more relationship-oriented because she chose more relationship-oriented descriptors than task-oriented descriptors. Nancy then placed an X in the box with the number 7 in it since that is how many relationship-oriented items she circled.

Before proceeding to item 2, go to page 28, where you will find the Connecting Style Survey Self-Scoring Grid, and select one behavior from each of the seven pairs under "Relationship-Oriented" and "Task-Oriented" by circling the number to the left of the behavior you choose. Then place an X in the box with the number that coincides with the total number of items circled under either "Task-Oriented" or "Relationship-Oriented," whichever is the higher number (just as Nancy did).

2. **Next, you'll determine whether your style is more *quietly assertive* or *forcefully assertive*, and to what extent.** Follow the same instructions as you did in item 1 above. Looking at the illustrations, Nancy selected five items under "Forcefully Assertive" and only two under "Quietly Assertive," so she put an X in the box marked "5" located on the right, or the "Forcefully Assertive," side of the vertical line.

Now go to page 28 again, and select one item on the Connecting Style Survey Self-Scoring Grid from each of the seven pairs under "Quietly Assertive" and "Forcefully Assertive" by circling the numbers next to the appropriate items. Place an X in the box with the number that coincides with the total number of items circled under either "Quietly Assertive" or "Forcefully Assertive," whichever is the higher number (just as Nancy did). Then draw an intersecting line to connect the two X's as illustrated and mark that point of intersection with an X.

NAME: NANCY   *CONNECTING STYLE SURVEY*
SCORING ILLUSTRATION

Connecting Style Survey

Self-Scoring Grid

Task-Oriented

1. **Information focused** (Pay attention to facts, data and the task at hand; when people react emotionally it makes me uncomfortable and is counterproductive to achieving the goal.)
2. **Less concerned with gaining approval and avoiding rejection**
3. **Control feelings**
4. **Serious, formal, less approachable on a personal level**
5. **Body language reveals limited range of emotions**
6. **Facial expression reveals limited range of emotions**
7. **Voice tone and variation reveal limited range of feelings**

Quietly Assertive

1. **More quiet** (More reserved and measured; keep a lot to myself; avoid the spotlight; don't like to force my ideas on a group.)
2. **Listen / reflect** (Conscious of not taking more than my share of time talking in a group; gather information and impressions and voice opinions once they are more clearly formulated.)
3. **Move less and slower**
4. **Talk softer and slower**
5. **Lean back when making a point**
6. **Less confrontational** (Pull back/ avoid when challenged or attacked.)
7. **Decide more carefully**

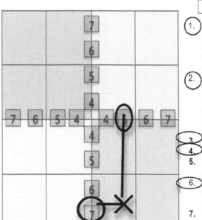

Forcefully Assertive

1. **More forceful** (More direct and certain; say what's on my mind; comfortable in the spotlight; urge others to accept my ideas.)
2. **Talk / act** (Have a lot to say and can take over a conversation if others let me; share my opinions even when others know more about the subject or topic.)
3. **Move more and faster**
4. **Talk louder and faster**
5. **Lean forward when making a point**
6. **More confrontational** (Push back/ confront when challenged or attacked.)
7. **Decide more quickly**

Relationship-Oriented

1. **People focused** (Pay attention to people's feelings, concerns and motivations; when people react emotionally it helps me to understand the whole story.)
2. **More concerned with gaining approval and avoiding rejection**
3. **Express feelings**
4. **Warm, open, approachable on a personal level**
5. **Body language reveals wide range of feelings**
6. **Facial expression reveals wide range of feelings**
7. **Tone and variation in my voice reveal wide range of feelings**

Connecting Style Survey

Self-Scoring Grid

Task-Oriented

1. **Information focused** (Pay attention to facts, data and the task at hand; when people react emotionally it makes me uncomfortable and is counterproductive to achieving the goal.)
2. **Less concerned with gaining approval and avoiding rejection**
3. **Control feelings**
4. **Serious, formal, less approachable on a personal level**
5. **Body language reveals limited range of emotions**
6. **Facial expression reveals limited range of emotions**
7. **Voice tone and variation reveal limited range of feelings**

Quietly Assertive

1. **More quiet** (More reserved and measured; keep a lot to myself; avoid the spotlight; don't like to force my ideas on a group.)
2. **Listen / reflect** (Conscious of not taking more than my share of time talking in a group; gather information and impressions and voice opinions once they are more clearly formulated.)
3. **Move less and slower**
4. **Talk softer and slower**
5. **Lean back when making a point**
6. **Less confrontational** (Pull back/ avoid when challenged or attacked.)
7. **Decide more carefully**

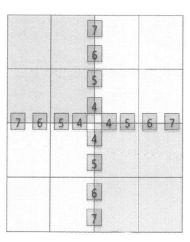

Forcefully Assertive

1. **More forceful** (More direct and certain; say what's on my mind; comfortable in the spotlight; urge others to accept my ideas.)
2. **Talk / act** (Have a lot to say and can take over a conversation if others let me; share my opinions even when others know more about the subject or topic.)
3. **Move more and faster**
4. **Talk louder and faster**
5. **Lean forward when making a point**
6. **More confrontational** (Push back/ confront when challenged or attacked.)
7. **Decide more quickly**

Relationship-Oriented

1. **People focused** (Pay attention to people's feelings, concerns and motivations; when people react emotionally it helps me to understand the whole story.)
2. **More concerned with gaining approval and avoiding rejection**
3. **Express feelings**
4. **Warm, open, approachable on a personal level**
5. **Body language reveals wide range of feelings**
6. **Facial expression reveals wide range of feelings**
7. **Tone and variation in my voice reveal wide range of feelings**

THE NAMES OF THE FOUR STYLE QUADRANTS

Each of the four quadrants represents a style. Write each one on the Connecting Style Self-Scoring grid as I describe each one below.

- The quadrant in the top left is called *Analytical.* People in this quadrant are more quietly assertive and task-oriented; the role most natural for them in a team setting is *critical thinker.*

- Moving to the right, people who fall in the next quadrant are more task-oriented, like the Analytical, but are more forcefully assertive. These people are referred to as *Drivers* and are comfortable in the *director* role.

- Continuing clockwise, people who fall into the next quadrant are more forcefully assertive, like Drivers, but are more relationship-oriented. These folks are referred to as *Energizers*—the role they like to play is *team builder.* Notice that Energizers and Analyticals share neither of the two personality attributes.

- Like Energizers, people in this next quadrant are more relationship-oriented, but like Analyticals they are more quietly assertive. Those who fit in this quadrant are *Supportives*—they are relationship-oriented and quietly assertive and commonly play the role of *team player.*

   Which style has no personality traits in common with the Supportive style? If you guessed Driver, you guessed correctly!

CHAPTER 5

YOUR SECONDARY STYLE

To identify your secondary style, copy the X on page 28 into the corresponding secondary style box within your style quadrant on page 33. Notice that the secondary style quadrants are named and organized in a pattern identical to the connecting style quadrants.

WHAT DOES YOUR SECONDARY STYLE MEAN?

Your secondary style is the one that describes you second best. When people from the same style interact among themselves, they take on the characteristics of their secondary style and their connecting style. Once I explain how secondary style is determined, you will hopefully see the logic behind this.

Your connecting style is determined by whether you are more relationship or task-oriented, combined with whether you are more forcefully or quietly assertive. It does not reflect the strength of your behavioral tendencies. Your secondary style is a reflection of degree.

In the example, Nancy, an Energizer, circled all seven relationship-oriented statements and no task-oriented statements, four forcefully assertive statements, and three quietly assertive statements, placing her in the Supportive secondary style quadrant. Nancy is much more relationship-orientated than task-oriented, but almost as quietly assertive as she is forcefully assertive. So we would assume that if she were interacting among a group of Energizers, she would probably be more relationship-oriented and quietly assertive than her same style peers. The style that is more quiely assertive and relationship-oriented is Supportive, and in fact, Nancy would probably gravitate toward the "team player" role of a Supportive when working among Energizers.

In which secondary style quadrant would an Energizer who is extremely forcefully assertive but only slightly more *relationship* than *task-oriented* fall? If you answered Driver, you would be correct. That individual would play the role of Energizer except when working with other energizers in which case she would come across like a Driver.

For about 25 percent of the population, secondary style is the same as primary style. These individuals have a very definite style and might have to work a little harder to activate behaviors common to the other three styles in order to fully engage people outside of their style.

For approximately another 25 percent of the population, secondary style is in one of the four interior boxes, which happens to be the opposite of their primary style. People with this profile have qualities associated with all four styles, which makes them naturally quite adaptable in that they can connect across all styles.

PRIMARY AND SECONDARY STYLES

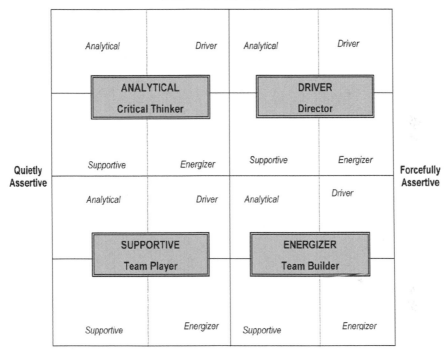

Connecting Style Validation

To make sure you are in the quadrant that best describes you, compare the descriptions below each style in the table "Connecting Styles: Common Characteristics" on the next page.

Designate the style that describes you best by placing the number "1" in the box next to that style. Place the number "2" in the box next to the style that describes you second best. This would be your secondary style. Now place the number "4" next to the style that is least like you. This is your opposite style. We'll get to that later.

Most of you will have found that your Connecting Style Survey results were spot on. Others of you may feel that one of the other three styles comes closer to describing you. Or perhaps you just can't decide which of two styles fits you best. How you think about your style at this moment is likely to change as you learn more about styles and yourself in the upcoming chapters. What really matters is optimizing your style versatility by learning to relate to, accept, and incorporate the best skill sets from all four styles.

CONNECTING STYLES: COMMON CHARACTERISTICS

☐ *ANALYTICAL—Critical Thinker*

Logical	Focused
Precise	Serious
Emotionally controlled	Private
Quietly determined	Methodical
Patient with complex challenges	Cautious

☐ *DRIVER—Director*

Strong-willed	Direct and to the point
Results-driven	Independent
Not easily influenced	Decisive
Takes charge quickly	Practical
Action-oriented	Impatient

☐ *ENERGIZER—Team Builder*

Social	Passionate
Full of ideas	Seeks approval
Fun	Restless
Stimulating	Bored with details
Promoting	Takes interesting detours

☐ *SUPPORTIVE—Team Player*

Good listener	Service-oriented
Open and sharing	Likes structured, stable settings
Modest	Cautious
Gets results	Dependable
Patient	Willing

White out any scores you placed in the boxes next to the styles on page 35. Then ask three to five people to review the common characteristics of each of the four styles and rank the styles from 1 (most like you) to 4 (least like you) to the right of the Connecting Style name. Where differences exist between your self-assessment and the rater's assessment of your style, explore with each rater the specific behavioral observations that led to the differences.

CONNECTING STYLE: QUESTIONS AND ANSWERS

The following are some of the most common questions people ask about the Connecting Style Survey followed by my answers:

1. **Question:** Doesn't personality typing lead to labeling, stereotyping, and putting people in a box?

   Response: The purpose of the Connecting Style Survey is not to put you in a box but to get you out of it. Everyone behaves in ways that reflect qualities of all four styles, but we each have one style that is most automatic, natural, and habit forming, a style that defines how we come across, perhaps more than we realize, especially under pressure or threat. By making you more aware of when you are in that box, the Connecting Style Survey helps you expand outside of that box and leads to style flexibility: the key to success.

2. **Question:** Does knowing your Connecting Style tell you what your strengths and weaknesses are so you can pursue careers that fit with your abilities?

   Response: Connecting Style does not define strengths and weak-nesses. People who share the same Connecting Style tend to share in common those skills, abilities, and roles in which they are most and least natural, find easiest and hardest to master, and to which they are most and least attracted. Although people tend to develop strengths and weaknesses that correspond to the areas in which they are most naturally adept, it is simply because it represents the path of least resistence.

Your Connecting Style does not set limits on what skills and capabilities you can master and what you can accomplish and contribute in any role using any skillset. With enough motivation, commitment, and persistence, you can become an expert in nearly anything. Once you've mastered a skill, how long it took you is no longer relevant.

3. **Question:** How accurately does Connecting Style predict success?

   Response: Connecting Style explains only some aspects of personality. In fact, many of the most powerful determinants of success are not explained by Connecting Style, including character (courage, morality, ethics, integrity, loyalty, honesty), mental well-being, discipline, drive, and interests.

4. **Question:** Two styles describe me almost equally well. I am more like a Driver at work and an Energizer at home. Am I an Energizer with a secondary style of Driver or a Driver with a secondary style of Energizer?

   Response: The best way to check if you are leaning more toward one or the other is to ask yourself which behaviors require more energy: those listed under Driver—like getting closure—or those listed under Energizer?" ("Oh—definitely the Driver behaviors take more energy.")

   "So your style is more toward the Energizer. The logic is that while you are very effective and spend lots of time in the Driver role, the Energizer role requires less energy and is more automatic. So Energizer is more your comfort zone.

But with that said, you still might feel on the fence about which style best describes you. The fact is that there are wide differences between people in how definite they are about their Connecting Style. Just as some people are a perfect size-eight shoe and others are between a seven-and-a-half and an eight-and-a-half, depending on the shoe, some identify instantly and fully with one Connecting Style and others fall between two styles. Others still, like me, are clear about their Connecting Style but are on the fence with regard to their secondary Connecting Style." (I am an Energizer for sure, but some days I think am more Energizer-Analytical, and others Energizer-Supportive. But I am definitely not Energizer-Energizer or Energizer-Driver.)

CHAPTER 6

TIPS FOR CONNECTING MORE EFFECTIVELY

This chapter contains descriptions of each Connecting Style and tips for connecting more effectively.

1. Read the two pages associated with your primary style and the two pages associated with your secondary style. In the *Connecting Style Description* subsections to follow, highlight those areas that resonate most with you. On the *Tips* pages, highlight those that best reflect the behavioral changes you want to make.

2. Select two to four of the behavioral changes you highlighted. Using the Development Plan Forms in Appendix B, create a development plan for each.

3. Read the pages describing the other two Connecting Styles as well.

ANALYTICALS (CRITICAL THINKERS)

Connecting Style Description

Analyticals, the most controlled and private of the four styles, are the hardest to read and get to know. Like everyone else, they have strong passions, opinions, and emotions, but since they are often uncomfortable sharing them, they risk being misread or misunderstood as cold, detached, or lacking enthusiasm.

Their focus on tasks, facts, and ideas is at the forefront of their working style. They spend much of their time gathering and analyzing data—asking a lot of questions about specific details. They appreciate structure and organization and take a systematic, detailed approach to communicating. The detailed approach and sometimes slow pace of the Analytical can be frustrating to the Driver and Energizer, who may tune out or want to jump in to help move the Analytical to act.

Of the four styles, Analyticals can be the most critical, the hardest on both themselves and others. They make excellent critical thinkers, often acting as the protector of data integrity on a team, but they can appear to be critical of others as they focus on solving the problem. Their opinions carry weight as their points of view appear to have been carefully considered. Finding merit and expressing appreciation do not come naturally to them, so when they do express appreciation or praise, it has a powerful effect.

Tips for Analyticals (Critical Thinkers)

- Express appreciation—find merit in others' words and actions; let people know how they have had a positive impact (for example, "You got me thinking," "Our discussion came in handy," "I quoted you the other day.").

- When you disagree, find a positive and valuing way to express it. Disagree only after you demonstrate that you find merit in some aspect of another's point.

- Share more of what you are thinking and feeling.

- Share something personal—especially with Supportives and Energizers.

- Show your reactions in the moment.

- Demonstrate more enthusiasm when interacting with others. Nod your head, smile, and use more inflection in your voice.

- Move more quickly and speak faster than you normally do. Act with enthusiasm!

- Reduce the amount of facts and figures in your conversations. Be more casual!

- Be aware of the body language of others. Adjust your communication in reaction to non-verbal communication.

- Spice up or shorten your delivery as you see your audience fading.

DRIVERS (DIRECTORS)

Connecting Style Description

Drivers are very strong communicators who don't hesitate to express opinions and form conclusions. Their certainty and organized thinking makes them compelling, and their direct to-the-point style adds to their credibility. They get people's attention and gain their confidence quickly. "She really knows what she is talking about."

But their desire for results often leads Drivers to rush to conclusions without properly vetting their assumptions or verifying facts. Under pressure, when they see a solution, their inclination is to get it done rather than ask questions like "Is this the best solution?" "What have I missed?" "Do I have all the facts?"

Their natural independence and confidence cause them to inadvertently exclude others from their decision-making process. Drivers often ask for input after they're already committed to their own ideas. At that point, input from others is marginalized.

Drivers are often surprised that others find them intimidating and defensive. They do not recognize the impatient, dismissive, unreceptive tone they frequently project. Drivers see themselves as open to feedback and when they don't receive any, assume it is because everyone agrees with their compelling point of view. In fact, not everyone shares the Driver's comfort with stating agreements/disagreements and openly debating issues. Often, others conclude that it's simply not worth disagreeing with a Driver. At best it's uncomfortable, and it can become a no-win situation when a Driver is acting as though he or she has little to learn from others. However, silence does not necessarily indicate agreement, and a Driver may pay for his or her assumptions when resistance or passive–aggressive reactions surface later.

Tips for Drivers (Directors)

- Make sure you are connecting with your audience based on their needs, concerns, and perspective.

- Check for understanding. Make sure you understand others, and they understand you. Paraphrase what you heard others say.

- Listen. Don't rush to solve problems, offer solutions, or judge right or wrong.

- Do not interrupt or pretend to listen until it is your turn to talk.

- Don't rush to implementation once you have a solution. It may not be the best solution. Encourage more input and feedback. You may unknowingly be communicating that you don't need or want other people's input.

- Avoid monopolizing the floor. Balance speaking with respectful listening to others.

- Express appreciation. Let people know the positive impact of their contribution.

- Ask questions. Energizers will easily share their ideas and opinions, and Analyticals will provide you with potentially important data if you ask them.

- Pay attention to feelings—your own and those of others—either expressed or unspoken.

- Ask for and accept help.

- Avoid projecting impatience or coming across as opinionated, and others will be more willing to share their opinions and ideas.

ENERGIZERS (TEAM BUILDERS)

Connecting Style Description

Energizers have an abundance of ideas and a powerful urge to set them free. Their energy and intense focus on their audience gives them a highly visible and powerful presence. A mutual connection is formed if their outward energy is complemented with equally powerful active listening, understanding, and appreciating of others.

Most Energizers have a healthy desire for recognition and approval. They strive to achieve it by sharing stories, ideas, jokes, advice, and wisdom. Only after they really understand the powerful impact that active listening has on engaging others are they sufficiently motivated to make a change in the sending-receiving balance.

Fortunately, Energizers have the makings of excellent listeners once they—and don't take this the wrong way—get over themselves. They have the unusual ability to understand what is said and the feelings behind the words. They can skillfully summarize and reflect what they hear as well.

When frustrated, Energizers can come across as angry and aggressive, sometimes without realizing how personally hurtful this can feel, especially to Supportives and Analyticals.

Tips for Energizers (Team Builders)

- Listen, listen, listen. Discipline yourself to filter what you say and how much you talk, based on your audience's style and receptivity as expressed through their body language.

- Speak more succinctly. State your premise and then elaborate with essential details.

- Pause more frequently. Count to three after the other person finishes before jumping in.

- Draw others out: Invite them to speak.

- Practice active listening and reflect back what you heard.

- Make statements in a more provisional way. If you sound too certain, it discourages others from giving their opinions.

- Work on becoming more organized and prepared.

- Make sure your audience understands you. Do they need more detail, examples, and specifics?

- Stay on topic and stick to the schedule.

- Calibrate how formal or informal, touchy-feely, or task-focused your approach should be based on the needs of your audience.

- Be very careful not to attack or criticize others when frustrated, either directly through sarcasm or indirectly with body language. It can result in people becoming defensive and annoyed. More than any other style, Energizers need to make sure they don't overreact emotionally.

SUPPORTIVES (TEAM PLAYERS)

Connecting Style Description

Supportives are typically warm, friendly, and cooperative. They enjoy working with and helping others. Relationships are extremely important to Supportives, who will do what they can to build and/or strengthen them. They try to accommodate the needs of others, dislike self-promotion, and prefer to avoid confrontation. However, Supportives risk being taken advantage of due to their easygoing nature. It is sometimes difficult to know what lies beneath the friendly and accommodating surface of the Supportive. So, it's up to Supportives to share their opinions and communicate what they need, or to express when they are uncomfortable with someone else's behavior.

Of the four styles, Supportives are naturally the best listeners. They are genuinely interested in others, open-minded, moderate in their criticism, and appreciative of friendly interaction. The challenge for Supportives is getting their point across, especially because the other three styles don't make it easy for Supportives to speak their minds. If Supportives want to be treated with respect, they must learn to jump in and even ruffle feathers occasionally.

Supportives' ability to make others feel special, accepted, cared about, understood, included, valued, respected, and trusted is critical to their success as leaders. Through the relationship, Supportives can bolster confidence and self-esteem in others that leads them to accomplish things they never thought possible. The depth and endurance of their impact seems to be tied to the feeling that "He or she believed in me when no one else would . . . or always saw the best in me, even when I couldn't see it myself."

Tips for Supportives (Team Players)

- Be more direct in requesting what you need from others. Don't assume people can read your mind or that they will be responsive to your needs just because you are responsive to theirs.

- Share your opinions more frequently. Don't wait to be asked. Energizers and Drivers may not always make it easy for you to claim your share of "air time," so you may have to push a little harder than people have seen you do.

- Praising others is a relatively safe and highly underutilized way to show self-confidence in your opinions. For example, "I really like how this is written. . . . You make an excellent point. . . . I am proud of our team's performance today."

- Make sure your posture, tone of voice, and eye contact match the assertive tone of your message.

- Be aware of undoing your assertive messages by minimizing their importance. For example, don't say, "This may sound silly but . . . don't worry, it's no big deal." And don't apologize by saying, "I hope you're not mad at me."

- Try to avoid cleaning up other people's messes and taking on roles others want to avoid.

- Avoid the tendency to take on assignments without making sure you have the clarity, resources, and support necessary to do them well. Use your right to ask questions if you are confused.

- Supportives feel very uncomfortable taking credit or promoting themselves. Instead supportives rely on the hope that they will get the recognition they deserve based on the effort they put in. It's up to you to make people aware of your value.

- Don't let unspoken resentment build up. People will respect you more for asking more of them, and they will appreciate not having to read your mind.

- Allow other people to help you once in a while.

CHAPTER 7

CONNECTING ACROSS STYLES

*"Everything that irritates us about others
can lead us to an understanding of ourselves."*

—CARL JUNG, SWISS PSYCHOLOGIST (1875–1961)

People have a tendency not only to prefer their own style over others, but also to be intolerant of the behaviors associated with the other styles, especially the styles least like their own. As you may expect, cross-style biases are strongest among people whose primary and secondary connecting styles are one and the same, whereas those whose secondary styles are the opposite of their primary styles are most tolerant of other styles. During workshops, when different style teams give each other feedback, it's rare to hear much genuine appreciation for each other's differences. Instead, there is an underlying tone of superiority suggesting that if the other style groups "behaved more like us, they would be much more effective, our relationships would be better, and we would produce better results." People seem genuinely baffled as to why the other styles would be partial to their own way of doing things.

It is unusual to see someone move out of the comfort zone of their own style to connect across styles. Most people keep behaving the same way, while harboring frustration about the annoying habits of those with other styles. What they don't see is how one style's behavior causes those with another style to harden their own defining habits. The following cartoons illustrate this phenomenon.

Driver to Analytical

DRIVER   **ANALYTICAL**

Analytical to Driver

ANALYTICAL   **DRIVER**

The Ah Ha! Moment

Promoting our style of connecting *pushes* others deeper into their connecting style. THE KEY TO CONNECTING ACROSS STYLE IS TO...

ANALYTICAL   SUPPORTIVE   ENERGIZER   DRIVER

MIRROR THEIR STYLE AND THEY WILL CHANGE!

No matter how well intentioned you are, judging and demeaning other people's styles only makes them feel more defensive and set in their approach. Fortunately, there is a simpler way to encourage someone with a different style to modify rather than harden their behavior. Can you guess what that approach is? Find the answer on the top of the next page.

MIRRORING EACH STYLE

If you work with . . .	Then . . .	And they will . . .
Analyticals	Be prepared, organized, and methodical. Stick to business and to the facts.	Relax and be more decisive.
Drivers	Be direct and clear. Stay focused on getting results and supporting the goal.	Be more inclusive.
Supportives	Be considerate of people's feelings. Express personal interest and warmth.	Share their opinions.
Energizers	Ask for their input and listen to their ideas. Allow for socializing and express appreciation.	Move more quickly toward implementation.

In the next chapter you will find much more detailed advice about how to apply these principles to connect with people across styles.

CHAPTER 8

GUIDELINES FOR CONNECTING WITH EACH STYLE

This chapter provides specific, practical advice for successfully engaging people of each style. There is one page per style. The upper half of the page lists the common characteristics associated with that style in great detail. The bottom half lists the behaviors that will engage people of that style (on the left) and the behaviors to avoid because they are likely to be off-putting (on the right).

Readers have reported that these pages are great to review prior to a meeting or an interaction with someone whose style you can pretty well guess.

ANALYTICALS (CRITICAL THINKERS)

Common Characteristics

- Task-focused
- Less assertive
- Quietly determined, focused
- Loyal
- Seek autonomy and control
- Excellence-driven, perfectionists
- Intellectually oriented
- Patient with complex challenges
- Good problem-solvers
- Analytical
- The quietest type
- Emotionally controlled
- Serious
- Sticklers on fairness
- Private—rarely let their guard down
- Methodical and precise
- Talk slowly and quietly
- Cautious risk takers
- Cautious decision makers
- Appreciate clarity, consistency, planning
- Sparing with appreciation and compliments
- Finish what they start (eventually)
- Critical

Engage Analyticals By . . .

- Preparing your case in advance
- Respecting their privacy, space, and time
- Going through a methodical decision-making process: listing the pros and cons
- Contributing in a specific role with clear expectations for how you plan to add value
- Drawing up a step-by-step approach with no surprises
- Relying on an organized, fact-based presentation of your argument
- Planning sufficient time to do an excellent job with professional courtesies

Avoid . . .

- Being disorganized or undisciplined
- Spending time on personal issues, being too talkative or emotional
- Moving too quickly to solutions
- Being unclear about your value, role, and contributions
- Leaving things to chance
- Whining
- Selling by manipulation or emotional appeal
- Taking shortcuts
- Pushing too hard with unrealistic deadlines

DRIVERS (DIRECTORS)

Common Characteristics

- Task-focused
- More assertive
- Always driving toward results
- Quickly take charge and initiative
- Decisive
- Direct and to the point
- Strong points of view
- Hard working
- Thick skinned
- Confident
- Strong managers and people coordinators
- Willing to challenge others' ideas
- Responsible and dependable
- Independent
- Action oriented
- Low tolerance for advice and direction

Engage Drivers By . . .

- Showing mental toughness
- Demonstrating loyalty
- Being disciplined
- Being focused on winning
- Hard work and sacrifice
- Being self-reliant
- Being direct
- Arriving at meetings prepared with a structured results-focused agenda
- Not being intimidated
- Standing up for and protecting the people on your team
- Presenting in a clear, fact-based fashion relevant to the Driver's goals and concerns
- Giving up without a fight
- Emotional overreaction
- Being disorganized or unprepared
- Unrealistic ideas not directly connected to winning
- Giving them bad news directly
- Providing them alternatives that allow them to make decisions
- Persuading with evidence
- Being on time

Avoid . . .

- Long explanations
- Letting others do your work
- Using jargon
- Acting pretentious
- Blaming others
- Going over their heads or around them to get your way
- Excuses, complaining, whining, or pouting
- Being overly sympathetic, nurturing, or touchy-feely in how you contact them
- Taking criticism personally
- Going off on tangents

ENERGIZERS (TEAM BUILDERS)

Common Characteristics

- People-focused
- More assertive
- Like to express and sell their ideas to others
- Have an overabundance of ideas
- Most visionary style
- Bold
- Inspiring
- Best networkers
- Think out loud
- Love fun, humor, and spontaneity
- Like to lift others' morale
- Openly express feelings and opinions
- Impulsive, can bite off more than they can chew
- Competitive with high energy— will almost wear you out
- Want approval and recognition
- Risk takers
- Can be direct in feedback, occasionally abrasive
- Jump from one activity to another

Engage Energizers By . . .

- Allowing them to talk about their vision and ideas without judging them
- Being in the moment or spontaneous, going with the flow
- Allowing for relating and socializing
- Being a good active listener
- Asking for their input and ideas
- Expressing appreciation
- Letting them know what you are feeling and thinking
- Having fun
- Discussing how to apply their ideas to address important challenges and benefit people

Avoid . . .

- Challenging or debating as it can quickly turn into an argument
- Marginalizing or ignoring their contributions
- Reeling in the conversation to focus on pragmatics too soon
- Being aloof or deadpan
- Making them feel excluded or unimportant
- Being cold and impersonal
- Being critical
- Going strictly "by the book"

SUPPORTIVES (TEAM PLAYERS)

Common Characteristics

- People-focused
- Less assertive
- Team-oriented
- Appreciative
- Quiet friendliness
- Accommodating, helpful, supportive
- Good listeners
- Relationship builders
- Open and sharing
- Withhold critical feedback
- Modest
- Can appear calm even when a storm rages within
- Appreciate clarity and direction
- Industrious
- Implementers
- Service-oriented
- Like structured, stable settings
- Reluctant to use authority
- Cautious decision makers

Engage Supportives By . . .

- Expressing personal interest, warmth, and attention to relationships
- Expressing appreciation
- Being a good listener
- Including the people-related issues when you present your case
- Being organized and structured in your approach and respectful of their time
- Paying attention to their becoming quiet or overly accommodating (This may be a sign of concealed anger, and they may need to be drawn out.)
- Approaching decisions in a participative fashion

Avoid . . .

- Sticking coldly to business
- Taking them for granted
- Forcing the conversation toward quick decisions related to your objectives
- Being too focused on numbers and facts and not attending to the impact of plans on people
- Being disorganized, inconsistent, or confusing in how you approach your working relationship
- Bullying or being excessively abrasive or sarcastic
- Becoming angry and critical
- Being overcontrolling or autocratic
- Avoiding direct confrontation and direct expressions of anger

CHAPTER 9

INCREASING ROLE VERSATILITY

In the following table, place a plus sign (+) next to the role that is most natural for you and a minus sign (–) next to the role that is least natural for you. Hopefully, identifying the role you are least comfortable playing will spur you toward mastering that role. You should work to surround yourself with people who are comfortable playing the roles that you are least comfortable playing.

Connecting Style	Team Role	Plus or Minus
Analytical	Critical Thinker	
Driver	Director	
Energizer	Team Leader	
Supportive	Team Player	

Most of us too easily dismiss the possibility that we can be effective in roles outside of our styles. We say to ourselves, "Me, a Driver, become a team player in a team situation? Why, that's impossible!" Or is it? The following questions are intended to help you explore the barriers to playing a new and unfamiliar role, rethink some of the beliefs you've been harboring about your limitations, and challenge you to work on new behaviors that will help you become more effective in your least preferred role.

1. Think of a situation you are facing in which your optimum performance requires that you play the role you are least comfortable with. The situation may be one you are facing currently or will be facing in the future. It can even be a situation from the past, especially if you found it difficult.

2. What aspects of that role would be hardest for you and why? Be as specific as you can.

   Example A: "I am definitely a take-charge woman. I am captain of the swim team, editor of the school newspaper, and active in leadership roles in many other organizations. I am on a committee with other club presidents, and we often have brainstorming meetings in which I need to play the role of *Supportive (Team Player)*. I am not always a good listener and can get very impatient with people who don't 'get it' right away. I am quick to challenge rather than accept ideas at first. I am a very direct person and feel like a phony when I make supportive comments to people when I don't feel they deserve them. I can be very critical, and it shows. Also, when brainstorming, it is important to ask questions, and I am more comfortable giving my opinion."

   Example B: "Normally, I prefer working by myself or with a few friends who share my interests in technology, chess, and race cars. However, I am a volunteer EMT, and there are definitely times I have to play the role of Driver (Director). I don't feel comfortable giving orders, even though it is necessary when I am in emergency situations. I also like to think things through and would be nervous about making quick decisions on behalf of my team. I am concerned that people would not like me or would blame me for making the wrong decisions."

Situation:

_____

_____

_____

_____

_____

The role you will be playing:

_____

_____

_____

_____

_____

Aspects of the role that will be most challenging and why:

_____

_____

_____

_____

_____

Now underline all the behaviors and habits that you will either have to start doing, stop doing, or do more of or less of to enable you to effectively play that role. Enter the behaviors you underlined in the left-hand column in the Expanding My Role Worksheet on the facing page. Use the following Sample Worksheet below as an illustration to guide you.

EXPANDING MY ROLE—SAMPLE WORKSHEET

Role I am committed to developing: DIRECTOR

Do *less* of or *stop* doing	Commitment	Qualities I can apply
Concerned that people will not like me or blame me	I will not let my concern that people will like me less or blame me keep me from giving my opinions and making decisions.	Courage, discipline, patience

Do *more* of or *start* doing	Commitment	Qualities I can apply
Giving people orders	In emergencies, I will direct people I am responsible for, even if it feels uncomfortable.	Articulate, precise, even tempered
Making quick decisions	I will make decisions even if I do not have all the information I would normally want.	Courage, well-informed, analytical, methodical

EXPANDING MY ROLE—WORKSHEET

Role I am committed to developing:

Do *less* of or stop doing	Commitment	Qualities I can apply

Do *more* of or start doing	Commitment	Qualities I can apply

CHAPTER 10

CONNECTING FROM YOUR SWEET SPOT

J ust as everybody has a preferred style or comfort zone, everybody has a sweet spot—*the behavioral approach with which we
engage and influence others with maximum intended impact.*

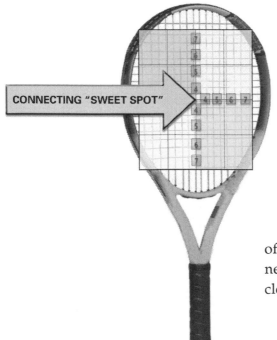

CONNECTING "SWEET SPOT"

The detailed diagram
of the sweet spot on the
next page zooms in for a
closer look.

YOU

+

A Modest Helping
of Your Opposite
Style's Perspective
and Habits

=

YOUR SWEET
SPOT

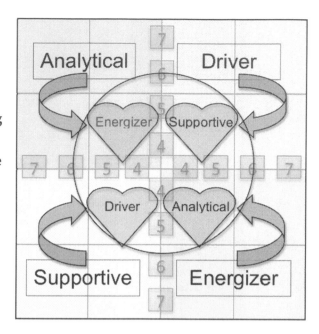

Impact of incorporating opposite-style behavior for each style	
When Analyticals get energized they… -Express their feelings and thoughts more openly -Express appreciation and praise -Are more open minded and flexible -Make decisions and take actions more quickly -Convey passion and enthusiasm -Smile, socialize, drop by to say hi -Present less detail, more big picture	**When Drivers are supportive they…** -Slow down, invite and include -Ask for directions and help -Express appreciation -Put others at ease -Share feelings, needs and human side -Admit mistakes -Delegate and support
When Supportives are Driving they… -Take risks and act on their instincts -Voice their opinion, even if others disagree -Deal with unreasonable requests -Present with appropriate confidence -Let others clean up their own mess -Pay attention to their own needs -Hold people to their promises	**When Energizers are analytical they…** -Are more focused and succinct -Stay with a task until completion -Are more private, discreet and respectful of personal boundaries -Are more cautious and thoughtful -Listen and ask questions -Respect time and don't over-commit -Plan and prepare

THE YIN AND THE YANG

Operating from your sweet spot not only allows you to be yourself, but it amplifies your natural strengths by bringing in contrasting perspectives, habits, and behaviors. When you incorporate the perspective and behavior of your opposite style, your message will have greater impact, consistent with what you intend. Unlike win-lose techniques designed to achieve a hidden agenda by manipulating your audience and exploiting their vulnerabilities, the behavioral modifications suggested by the Connecting Style model serve to make visible to your audience the important parts of who you are that are not immediately apparent. It enables people to see an even more honest picture of who you are and what you are trying to get across.

Isn't it ironic that the key to optimal effectiveness for each style is to act like those whose style can push our buttons most? Still, you will see just how much more powerful a connection we make when we season our comfort zone behavior with the defining habits of our opposite style. After all, the behaviors of our opposite style have more of what we are missing than any other style! A few examples that illustrate how this works follows:

Drivers are most effective when they connect in a personally supportive and inclusive way. When I was in my first corporate job, I got a phone call at home from my boss. It was all of about forty seconds in duration, but the impact was deep and long lasting. "Steve, it's Howard. Listen, I read your report and was really impressed. Some of the points you made never would have occurred to me, and I think it will really make a difference with the client. So thanks." The impact had a lot to do with the fact that Howard is a Driver.

When a Driver shows appreciation typical of a Supportive—the opposite style—nothing could be more empowering to the receiver. The very fact that it comes from the opposite style is what makes it so powerful. Knowing how infrequently Howard expressed appreciation gave his words that much more impact in boosting my self-confidence. It also led me to see him as much more engaging and personally invested in me, which in turn strengthened my loyalty to him.

In an interview with the *New York Times*, Richard Anderson, Chief Executive Officer of Delta Airlines and obviously a Driver, describes his most important leadership lessons and how he put them into practice. Notice in the examples he describes that the changes he made were essentially the incorporation of Supportive habits into his comfort zone behavior:

> I've learned to be patient and not lose my temper. . . . We have a tendency in these jobs to push really, really hard and want to go really, really fast. Change can't ever be fast enough. But you do have to be patient enough and make sure that you always remain calm. . . . You've got to be thankful to the people who get the work done, and you've got to be thankful to your customers. So, I find myself, more and more, writing hand-written notes to people.
>
> (How do you run meetings?) I want the debate. I want to hear everybody's perspective, so you want to try to ask more questions than make statements. . . . If it gets "uncollegial," we actually have a bell you can ring, in the conference room. . . . It's a violation of the rules of the road. So you ring the bell if something wasn't a fair shot, and we all laugh.[4]

Did you also notice that the changes he described were effective and enduring? Drivers will incorporate new habits once experience teaches them how much more effectively they can achieve important and tangible improvements.

It wasn't until Marc Cenedella, founder and CEO of The ladders.com, left a private equity firm to head up HotJobs that he discovered the enormous advantage of engaging versus directing people to optimize company performance. Cenedella captured the essence of how incorporating Supportive connecting strengths enables Drivers like him to successfully engage people in a 2010 interview with *New York Times* columnist Adam Bryant:

So the management style that I have is first, share your passion. Explain to people why it's an exciting idea and how they can be involved in it. . . . Really engaging people in that big picture is way more important, I think, to success.

Let me say something that's going to sound surprising. As C.E.O. today, I actually can't get anything done. So if I have a really good idea and I go tell people, 'Hey, you have to go do this,' or I impose it on them, people wonder, what does he really mean? It's open to so much misinterpretation and confusion that actually you're doing more harm for the organization than you are good. So the job of the C.E.O. becomes, "Hey everybody, what are everybody's good ideas? O.K., and what's yours? That's awesome. What do you think of that? Hmm, now anybody have a different view?

As human beings, we're not emotionally and anthropologically different from who we were on the plains of Africa 100,000 years ago. We need to feel that hey, I'm in a community.[5]

Supportives, who are naturally very strong relationship builders, face the opposite challenge. When they connect with the confidence that Drivers exude effortlessly, they make the most transformational leaders. If a Supportive feels arrogant when trying on this new role, it means it is probably being done right. It is not going to be comfortable. But it is going to let people know that they are strong, credible, and gutsy. The leader I most admired and the one who was the most highly rated (by people at all levels) was a Supportive named Phil. Phil was the youngest general manager in the history of the broadcast company that employed him. He was extremely knowledgeable about the business, passionate about the station, and very committed to the vision and values when it came to people. He made himself available to employees who wanted to share their ideas, and this quality made employees feel valued, included, and empowered to do their jobs, no matter what their level. What differentiated his leadership was that he was willing to stand up to those on his team who violated these principles when they dealt with other employees. He would not tolerate anyone being "thrown under the bus," and he modeled his principles when he stood up for his employees to senior executives, even when it put him at some risk.

Supportives assert their leadership through teaching, coaching, and mentoring. People who have been led by Supportives often describe the relationship as personally transformative.

Because of the patience, acceptance, optimism, and warmth with which Supportives connect, they can help people see the best in themselves and neutralize the self-criticism that damages self-esteem and leads to giving up. But Supportives have to first demonstrate the ability to be firm and demonstrate the courage of their convictions in order to gain the credibility and trust of such individuals.

The competitive edge of a Supportive-led team comes from the strong social values that Supportives instill, along with the discipline to live by those values. As quintessential team players, Supportive leaders create team-first cultures and tap into the powerful human instinct to fight harder for family and community than one would for his or her own self-interest. Winning for winning's sake, ego, power, or vanity is discouraged by Supportive leaders. Supportives are the anti–Gordon Gecco (*Wall Street's* "Greed is good") in that principles come first and power a vehicle to support those principles.

UCLA Bruins basketball coach John Wooden was said to never talk in terms of winning. His coaching and teaching were first and foremost a means of making his students and players better people. And yet, win they did. This Supportive-Driver was perhaps the winningest college basketball coach in history. His teams won eighty-eight consecutive games—still an unbroken record. In ten of his last twelve years as coach, UCLA won the NCAA championship. But what set him apart were the hundreds of lives he touched.

Wooden lived and taught straight from the Supportive rulebook, but he also managed to be a leader among leaders in a Driver culture. Wooden's Supportive core is reflected in the excerpts from his 1996 interview with the Academy of Achievement:

I think [basketball is] becoming too much showmanship and I don't like that. If I want showmanship, I'll go see the Globetrotters. In the pros today, the player that I'd rather see than anybody else is John Stockton from Utah, the all-time leader in assists. It's not just because he's the all-time leader in assists. It's his demeanor. He's a spirited player but never gets mad. He's quick, he's intelligent, he's unselfish and he can do all things. . . .

It's a beautiful game when it's played as a team. To me, it's not beautiful when it's an individual working one on one and going out and making a fancy dunk. . . .

Show those under your supervision that you really care for them. And that you're interested in the group as a whole, but also in them individually. One of my favorite coaches, Amos Alonzo Stagg, once said he never had a player he did not love. He had many he didn't like and didn't respect, but he loved them just the same. I hope my players know that I love them all.[6]

Energizers hit their sweet spot when they temper their natural ability to engage, motivate, and inspire with the focused, reasoned, and methodical approach of an Analytical. Energizers can speak to a packed audience and make each person feel they are speaking directly to him or her. But over time, Energizers must back up their emotional appeal with data and evidence. Like Analyticals, they need to demonstrate that they have also considered long-term implications and vetted their conclusions with the cold, hard, objective analysis of an actuary.

Energizers are most comfortable being spontaneous and going with the flow. But when their impulsive, emotionally driven side is balanced by a capacity to tolerate frustration, feel an urge to act without acting on it, and delay short-term gratification for longer-term success, they hit their sweet spot. Fun, excitement, passion, and responsible behavior create an unbeatable formula.

Energizers are very original and innovative, and they are constantly thinking outside of the box. They also can find themselves operating outside of the bounds of schedules, budgets, their designated role, other peoples' rules, and their due dates. Thus, as a leader, they can be very hard to follow unless they exercise the Analytical discipline and strong regard for personal boundaries, privacy, consistency, and efficiency.

Energizers are the most entertaining style; Analyticals are the most serious. Humor and fun are part of everyday life, but Energizers need to demonstrate that they take seriously the things that are important to those around them. It is what gives them the gravitas to offset their natural temperament and optimize their influence.

Last but not least is the importance of demonstrating that Energizers can shift into the Analytical-like listening role—taking things in quietly and thoughtfully, asking good questions, and listening in a way that makes people feel understood, valued, and included.

Perhaps the best illustration of how one moves from comfort zone to sweet spot comes from Energizer Robin Williams in a 2009 interview with Charlie Rose[7], during which he shared the two lessons he believed most responsible for his evolution from standup/ television comic to great dramatic actor. "It was the first day of shooting and I improvised a line and he (director George Roy Hill) made a face like this (grimace) and I said 'not good?' And he said, 'No. Just say the lines and commit to them.' That was the first great lesson. Second great lesson came from Peter Weir (who said) 'You know you have great power listening. That's the second part of the equation. When you listen to someone it's quite fascinating. And stillness is very powerful.' Second great lesson."

Analyticals are most effective when they connect emotionally, like an Energizer. When Analyticals reveal their feelings or show an interest in the needs and feelings of others, they move closer to their sweet spot. Others connect to them when Analyticals simply own up to their imperfections, worries, and fears.

Analyticals need to be more social and show interest in the relationships and lives of others, since they can come across as cold, uninterested, and critical. That can be intimidating, especially to

Energizers and Supportives, who have higher relationship needs. Connecting through relationships will warm people up and, often, motivate them to spend more time focusing on the substance of Analyticals' work.

Analyticals focus on the quality of the work and believe that one's work should speak for itself. Although they may find "selling" distasteful, in order to get others excited about their ideas, Analyticals need to focus more on creating a receptive audience and connecting with them.

Jacob Weisberg's article "Only Connect!" describes Barack Obama's Analytical style:

> His relationship with the world is primarily rational and Analytical rather than intuitive or emotional. . . . His tendency to focus on substance can make him seem remote and technocratic. So while many people continue to deeply admire him, few come away from any encounter feeling closer to him. He is not warm, he is not loyal, he is not deeply involved with others. . . .[8]

Maureen Dowd's comparison of Sarah Palin's Energizer and Barack Obama's Analytical style illustrates the powerful impact of incorporating qualities of your opposite style on leadership effectiveness:

> Palin can be stupefyingly simplistic, but she seems dynamic. Obama is impressively complex but he seems static.
>
> She nurtures her grass roots while he neglects his.
>
> He struggles to transcend identity politics while she wallows in them.
>
> As he builds an emotional moat around himself, she exuberantly pushes whatever she has, warts and all—the good looks, the tabloid-perfect family, the Alaska quirkiness, the kids with the weird names.
>
> This Visceral One never doubts herself. The Cerebral One welcomes doubt.

He's a highly intelligent man with a highly functioning West Wing, and he's likable, but he's not connecting on the gut level that could help him succeed.[9]

To underscore the point that style dynamics cut across political and racial affiliations, African-American liberal movie director Spike Lee, an Energizer, recently implored President Obama to "One time, go off! If there's any one time to go off, this is it, because this is a disaster" (referring to the BP Oil Spill).[10]

CHAPTER 11

ASSESSING CONNECTING STYLE IN OTHERS

Effectively communicating across styles requires the ability to accurately assess the Connecting Style of others, whether you are preparing for an interview, an attorney selecting jury members, a sales person making cold calls, a primary school teacher with twenty-five students and forty or fifty parents, or a phone support provider who may speak to hundreds of stressed-out people every day, you often have only a few minutes to figure out the style of the individual with whom you are dealing and limited information to go on. One of the advantages of the Connecting Styles model is that you can determine style based on immediately observable behavioral characteristics. With some people, these qualities jump out at you right away and their Connecting Style becomes obvious. But even when dealing with those whose distinguishing behaviors are not as clearly defined (which is about half the time), you can almost always narrow it down to two styles, which still gives you valuable insight about how best to approach the interaction.

Recognizing Connecting Style is easiest when you identify the other person's *assertiveness* and *task/relationship* orientation separately, rather than jumping ahead to guess their overall style. The following tables describe the observable behaviors that differentiate these two attributes.

QUIETLY OR FORCEFULLY ASSERTIVE?

Observable Behavior	Quietly Assertive	Forcefully Assertive
Amount of talking	Less	More
Rate of talking	Slower	Faster
Talking volume	Softer	Louder
Body movement	Less, slower	More, faster
Posture	Relaxed/Leans back	Leans forward

TASK- OR RELATIONSHIP-ORIENTED?

Observable Behavior	Task-Oriented	Relationship-Oriented
Uses facial animation	Less	More
Uses voice variation	Less	More
Uses animated gestures	Less	More

CONNECTING STYLE ASSESSMENT EXERCISE

You can practice assessing Connecting Style in others by trying to determine which of the four styles best fits the celebrities listed below.

Directions:

Using the two preceding tables, along with the style chart on page 24 to guide you, fill in the answers on the following matrix to determine each person's Connecting Style (the first example illustrates the concept; answers follow). Assess each celebrity separately starting with column one, "Forcefully or Quietly Assertive" then Relationship- or Task-Oriented and finally filling in the Connecting Style. The answers can be found on the following page.

Celebrity	Forcefully or Quietly Assertive	Relationship- or Task-Oriented	Connecting Style
1 Oprah Winfrey	Forcefully	Relationship	Energizer
2 Barack Obama			
3 Jimmy Fallon			
4 Bill Clinton			
5 Jack Nicholson			

Answers:

Celebrity	Forcefully or Quietly Assertive	Relationship- or Task-Oriented	Connecting Style
1 Oprah Winfrey	Forcefully	Relationship	Energizer
2 Barack Obama	Quietly	Task	Analytical
3 Jimmy Fallon	Quietly	Relationship	Supportive
4 Bill Clinton	Forcefully	Relationship	Energizer
5 Jack Nicholson	Forcefully	Task	Driver

PART THREE

Connecting Skills

CHAPTER 12

CONNECTED LISTENING

"Yeah, I called her up; she gave me a bunch
of crap about me not listening to her or something.
I don't know. I wasn't really paying attention."
—HARRY IN THE 1994 MOVIE *DUMB AND DUMBER*

Few experiences create a more powerful connection than listening with interest, openness, and empathy and giving the speaker the feeling that you understand what it's like to be in their shoes—in other words, that you "get them." Also known as "active listening," connected listening directly or indirectly contributes to satisfying all six basic connecting needs—the need to feel understood, valued, included, respected, empowered, and trusting. As discussed in Chapter 2, satisfying these needs lays the foundation for engagement and receptivity to the listener and whatever they happen to be selling (meant in the best way).

The influence you can achieve through connected listening is much more powerful and enduring than coersion, which works through threat and intimidation. In *Mind-Set Management: The Heart of Leadership*, UCLA management professor and clinical psychologist Sam Culbert explains the relationship between listening and influence:

You can tell people what you think is going on and what they need to do to operate effectively until you are blue in the face, but the only way to know what people . . . might be inclined to do differently based on your counsel, is to understand their mind-sets before you interact with them. . . . Comprehending the mind-set that is at the root of an individual's behavior is just the beginning. You must get it accurately, you must communicate to the other person that you have it straight, and you must actively relate to it prior to formulating your advice. Otherwise the advice you give will be aimed at solving problems that, in the other person's mind, either don't exist or exist in a different format than you are pursuing.[11]

The need to feel listened to and understood is every bit as basic and biological as the need for food, water, and sleep. The non-judgmental listening of a psychotherapist helps heal the effects of emotional abuse and damage, whereas the absence of listening—being ignored—causes emotional damage as evidenced by the pain of prolonged solitary confinement. In some societies, the punishment reserved for the most heinous crimes is the most severe form of ignoring—shunning. Over time, the individual shunned wanders off and dies.

And as powerful as listening is, good listeners are rare. Of the many hundreds of individuals I have worked with over the years, both in and out of the workplace, the most common complaint people express about each other is "(fill in the name) doesn't listen." In other words, we live in a world where everyone wants to be heard but nobody wants to listen.

Of the hundreds of senior executives I have coached, very few were considered skilled listeners by their colleagues. Although most were bothered by this feedback and even tended to agree, the rewards for being a skilled listener and consequences for poor listening does not rise to a level that motivates anyone to change. What we see of our leaders in the sound-bite dominated media is almost never the person in power listening—or anyone else for that matter.

Women tend to be better listeners than men on average. In newer industries, as the more male-dominated leadership model fades, more women move into leadership roles and the collaborative success model takes hold, listening has become increasingly important to career mobility and success.

Listening Conveys Strength

Listening, like empathy, is still associated with weakness and lack of decisiveness in the more hierarchical, male dominated organizations like the military. That's what U.S. Navy Captain Michael Abrashoff's impression was until he worked for Admiral William Perry. In *It's Your Ship: Management Techniques from the Best Damn Ship in the Navy,* Abrashoff writes about Perry:

> He was universally loved and admired by heads of state, by ministers of defense and foreign affairs, and by our own and our allies' troops. A lot of that was because of the way he listened. Each person who talked to him had his complete, undivided attention. Everyone blossomed in his presence, because he was so respectful, and I realized I wanted to affect people the same way. . . .
>
> It was painful, but crucial for my realization, that listening doesn't always come naturally to me. Perry opened my eyes to how often I just pretended to hear people. I wasn't paying attention; I was marking time until it was my turn to give orders.[12]

Ben Franklin recognized that listening to the other person's ideas plus resisting the urge to share your own pearls of wisdom creates the highest level of receptivity:

> Would you win the hearts of others, you must not seem to vie with them but to admire them. Give them every opportunity of displaying their own qualifications and when you have indulged their vanity they will praise you in turn and prefer you above others. Such is the vanity of mankind that

minding what others say is a much surer way of pleasing them than talking well ourselves.[13]

For an Energizer like Franklin, listening was an active struggle: "When another asserted something I thought in error, I denied myself the pleasure of contradicting him."[14] And while usually the smartest person in the room, he realized that "even the smartest comments would occasion envy and disgust."[15]

As long as good listeners are few and far between, you have a great opportunity to distinguish yourself by honing your listening skills.

The first step toward more effective listening is becoming aware of the most common forms of listening and the level of connection achieved by each.

Levels of Listening

Most listening is actually "me-focused," aimed at understanding information for our own purposes, to validate our beliefs and opinions, or listening for the right moment to break in and talk. But there is an even more disconnected level of listening that occurs far to frequently, which I refer to as "Barely Listening."

Barely Listening (Least Connected)

This is when the listener is consiously paying divided (as opposed to undivided) attention while you are talking: checking messages, signalling to people who walk by, eating lunch, and so on. I recently interviewed the controller of a senior residential care company as part of a culture change project initiated by the CEO. Before I could even introduce myself, he asked if I wouldn't mind his periodically checking for important emails. He reassured me that he was perfectly capable of doing both. No surprise that his observations and insights were as different from other people's perceptions as his policies and recommendations were disconnected from people's needs and the reality on the ground. An expert in everything, the return on investment in listening was no real benefit. Thinking back on this mercifully brief interaction reminds me that people who don't listen don't know how much they don't know. And those are the most dangerous people. Thankfully, this level of listening is rare. Far more common is listening while preoccupied about things that worry us.

Preoccuppied Listening

"Preoccuppied? Sorry, did you say preoccuppied? I was thinking about something else. Do you mind repeating it?"

In the era of multitasking, listening while preoccuppied has become accepted as the norm. Both are symptoms of a culture that values expedience and quantity over depth and quality. Research investigating the efficacy of multitasking demonstrates that the brain is not capable of doing more than one complex task at the same time. What appears to be simultaneously attending to more than one thing is actually alternating attention and filling in what you miss by guessing. The bottom line is that we are not capable of listening to two things at once. Listening with a busy mind cuts down considerably on even basic comprehension of the facts, let alone the underlying feelings and meaning.

But no matter how much we may be used to treating each other that way, we all know when someone is half-listening, and it feels no less disrespectful, rejecting, and devaluative as ever.

Self-Referential Listening

This is when people listen to share their story or opinion. At this level, you are listening through the filter of your experience and the opportunity to share your story or opinion. As you listen to other conversations, notice how frequently people alternate talking rather than respond to what each other is saying. While this kind of listening may be self-referential, it does demontrates that the listener is engaged in the conversation. But this form of listening tends to shift the focus from the understanding the other person's experience to the intersection between your experience and theirs.

Active Listening (Most Connected)

This most connected level of listening is aimed at understanding the listener for its own sake. While this may seem a bit unatural, when soley interested in understanding the other person, we naturally listen much more and differently, and respond in an entirely different way. We pay attention to the words, feelings, and what it means to that person. We organize what we hear, see, and intuit around formulating a full picture of their experience. Our goal is to make sure the other person feels understood. What we say and ask is all part of helping us to more accurately and deeply understand what we are hearing. Our evaluation of the merits of what they are saying, our own opinions, and even advice to what actions they may take is likely to be of little importance. This can't be accomplished without tuning out external competing demands for our attention and checking our understanding with the speaker along the way. This makes listening, which is typically a passive and invisible process, quite active. This can make a significant positive impact on the speaker, . . . is why connected listening is also referred to as "active listening."

Connected listening is used when the speaker is sharing a challenge, complaint, problem, or worry accompanied by defensiveness and emotions. People want to talk about what makes them really excited as well as upset. Often, a positive feeling can hide behind a negative feeling and sometimes it's the exact opposite. You never know what will unfold.

Active listening:

1. Empowers by maximizing the chance that the speaker will independently gain insight, clarity, and even discover solutions on their own.

2. Helps the speaker to develop and learn faster. People learn what they discover more and faster and retain it longer.

3. Leads to getting unstuck by creating a safe and uncluttered interspersonal space in which the speaker has the rare opportunity to

stay with a difficult conversation. Simply by eliminating criticism, solutions (premature), distractions, and shift of focus to others, the speaker will automatically begin to see the issues differently.

4. Gets to the root cause. When talking to someone who is active listening and demonstrating openness and positive regard for you, defensiveness melts away, allowing the speaker to become aware of aspects of a problem that are potentially embarassing or make them look weak. How often do discussions start out focused on blaming others for a problem and transition to what your contribution might have been and what you could have done differently—a much more actionable analysis?

5. Promotes self-esteem and confidence

What makes listening so powerful is the very fact that it helps the people we are listening to get behind their immediate opinions and reactions to the emotions and ideas that are driving them. It also lowers defensiveness and helps unlock rigidly held opinions and beliefs.

So far, we've talked about listening as the foundation to relationship building and communication effectiveness. The other reason listening is critical may be so obvious as to overlook it: You learn important things when you listen.

1. Which of the lower levels of listening do you recognize as part of your common pattern of interaction with others?

_____

_____

_____

2. How might your more frequent use of higher levels of listening benefit you and others?

_____

_____

_____

Good listening starts with an accurate self-assessment of your listening habits and identification of the skills you wish to develop. For this purpose, I have provided a Listening Habit Self-Assessment. Take a moment to read the directions and complete the following survey.

LISTENING HABIT SELF-ASSESSMENT

Directions for Scoring: Rate yourself on how often you demonstrate each of the following listening habits by placing an X in the appropriate box (Often, Sometimes, Rarely). Count the number of X's in each column and enter the total number in line 19. Multiply the number in line 19 by the number in line 20. Enter the result in line 21. Add together the three scores from line 21 and enter the total in line 22. Refer to the key following the survey to determine your level of effectiveness as a listener.

Listening Habits	Often (1)	Sometimes (2)	Rarely (3)
1. Listening with a clear mind and few distractions.			
2. Listening with attentive posture, eye contact, encouraging nonverbal feedback.			
3. Listening quietly.			
4. Letting a few seconds go by after another person stops talking before speaking.			
5. Using door openers to encourage the speaker to say more "Go on . . . I see . . . say more."			

Listening Habits	Often (1)	Sometimes (2)	Rarely (3)
6. Paraphrasing your understanding of what the speaker is saying, i.e., "So, you are having second thoughts about your decision..."			
7. Reflecting back what the speaker is feeling, i.e., "It sounds like this is really weighing heavily on your mind."			
8. Asking questions that focus on helping others talk it through—rather than on solving the problem for them.			
9. Genuine (as opposed to fake) listening.			
10. Totally tuning out competing stimuli like cell phones, texts, emails, etc.			
11. Not interrupting to say something you may think is more important.			
12. Not finishing others' sentences even if you think you know what they want to say.			
13. Not interrupting to agree or disagree.			
14. Not judging the importance or merit of what others are saying.			
15. Listening without formulating a rebuttal.			
16. Not interrupting to share your story ("I have it worse. . . .").			
17. Not asking irrelevant questions.			
18. Not moralizing (e.g., "Why did you do that?" "You brought it on yourself!").			
19. Subtotal			
20. Multiplier	x1	x2	x3
21. Score for Column			
TOTAL SCORE			

KEY	Score	Listening Effectiveness
	18–24	Highly effective
	25–34	Somewhat effective, but room for improvement
	35–42	Borderline effective and time for a tune up
	43–54	Barely listening, time for an overhaul

RECOMMENDATIONS FOR ALL FOUR STYLES

1. Being a good listener is at least as much about mindset as skill. Connected listening requires an attitude of genuine interest and belief that the speaker deserves your full attention. It requires being present and focused. This includes:

   a. hearing and "being with" whatever the speaker is saying with openness, acceptance, and compassion

   b. being aware of distracting thoughts, feelings, fantasies that arise, and distractions

   c. bringing your attention back to the speaker each time you notice you have drifted into your own thoughts

   d. noticing and managing any defensive reactions to what you hear, and the subsequent impulse to fight (criticize, moralize, lecture) or flee (withdraw, disengage)

2. Make sure the environment in which the discussion takes place is private, quiet, and free of interruptions and that you have ample time. Making a deliberate effort to create a listening-friendly environment sends a message that you respect and value the other person. Conversely, a "waiting-for-the-elevator" or hall meeting is apt to fail in getting your message across accurately and leaving the other person with a good feeling. Drivers and Energizers are often quite comfortable communicating in this fashion and Analyticals and Supportives are often uncomfortable communicating in this fashion.

The most common barriers to effective listening are:

1. Interrupting

2. Making suggestions about how to resolve the problem (without being asked)

3. Talking for the sake of talking rather than endure silences and pregnant pauses

4. Sharing your story

5. Finishing the other person's sentence

6. Interpreting the other person's behavior

CHAPTER 13

SELF-DISCIPLINE

"In reading the lives of great men, I found that the
first victory they won was over themselves . . .
self-discipline with all of them came first."

—HARRY S. TRUMAN, THIRTY-THIRD U.S. PRESIDENT (1884–1972)

Talent and desire make up the engine that drives success, but self-discipline is the steering wheel, brake, and accelerator. Comprised of the ability to delay immediate gratification to achieve longer-term success, overcome laziness and procrastination, and persevere over time and in the face of adversity, self-discipline is essential to directing your own path.

Imagine that you are four years old, with a plate of plump marshmallows sitting right in front of you. An adult tells you that he is leaving the room and that when he returns in several minutes, he will give you two marshmallows. But, if you don't feel like waiting, you can ring a bell any time, and he will return immediately and give you one marshmallow, but only one. What would you do? Would you go for the one marshmallow right away or wait for two?

This was exactly the predicament dozens of children found themselves in as participants in the now-famous study conducted in the 1960s at Stanford University by psychologist Walter Mischel. His "Marshmallow Study" is commonly cited as lending strong empirical support for the idea that impulse control and the ability to delay short-term gratification for long-term reward factors prominently in success—at least in school and the workplace.[16]

Subjects were followed up fourteen years later, at age eighteen. As expected, the students who delayed gratification during the initial study were more successful students later in life, as measured by higher SAT scores, better self-control and planning, and an ability to persevere in the face of minor setbacks.

For those of you who imagine your four-year-old selves giving in to temptation, as adults you probably have to work extra hard to discipline yourself. You may be more prone to going off on tangents, bypassing planning and preparation, taking shortcuts, and pulling things together last minute. You might also be susceptible to excessive partying, eating, and other forms of fun, and not being fully aware of the consequences of overindulging your fun zone.

For those who imagine your four-year-old selves successfully holding out for the two marshmallows, congratulations. Self-discipline is probably one of your strengths and has likely contributed to your success. But it is possible to overuse self-control and undermine your success, as in those who lean toward becoming compulsive or a perfectionist—a precursor to becoming a workaholic or a control freak, and even may lead to eating disorders such as anorexia and bulimia. Overcontrol can also interfere with the emotional openness essential to building strong relationships.

As adults, life can feel like the Marshmallow Study on steroids. Not only are we constantly struggling between short-term gratification and long-term success, but we are surrounded by a diversity of family and friends, many of whom seem determined to convince us to go for the one marshmallow instead of waiting for two. As I write this sentence, I wonder, *Should I take a break and do some shopping online (one marshmallow)? Or should I discipline myself to finish this section, which will make me feel much better about myself in the long run (two marshmallows)?* You'll never know whether I am writing this sentence immediately following the previous one, or after some online shopping. If I did have to account to another person for my decision to write or shop, it would have been much more likely that I would have followed through on what I committed to do.

Articulating your intention to yourself throughout the day can help keep your goals at the forefront. Other strategies to increase the attention you give to your intention and improve the odds of achieving your goal include:

- Mindfulness

- Discipline in one area leads to discipline in other areas

- A Goal-driven approach

- Measuring and monitoring your behavior and keeping records so progress can be tracked frequently

- Motivation

The fact that there is a relationship between Connecting Style and impulsivity should come as no surprise. Drivers and Energizers are naturally more impulsive, whereas Analyticals and Supportives are more self-disciplined. The following are just some of the countless "marshmallow" decisions we can find ourseves facing:

- Should I stay late and finish this project or work out at the gym?

- Should I review this report one more time for typos or print it out?

- Should I share gossip about one colleague with another or keep it to myself?

- Should I watch TV or prepare for tomorrow's meeting?

- Should I complain about how bored I am in this job or keep it to myself and see how I can make it more interesting?

- Should I move to a bigger home and live paycheck to paycheck, or stay where I am and save some money?

- Should I tell my colleague off now in front of everyone, or wait and think about a constructive approach to expressing my frustration?

The very high rate of business decision failure—at least 50 percent—is due to smart people impulsively implementing the first solution that seems to make sense (one marshmallow) rather than waiting until they understand the problem and its causes and implementing an effective solution (two marshmallows). Constant pressure for short-term results from the marketplace, media, shareholders, consumers, boards, and senior managers puts subtle pressure on all employees to implement any solution they can rather than hold off and implement the solution they should.

Self-discipline starts with becoming aware of the choices.

 How would you describe your strengths and weaknesses when it comes to self-discipline? Write down two strengths and two weaknesses below.

Strengths:

1. _____

   _____

2. _____

   _____

Weaknesses:

1. _____

   _____

2. _____

   _____

CHAPTER 14

HABIT CHANGE

*"It is never too late to become what
you might have been."*

—GEORGE ELIOT, AUTHOR (1819–1880)

The ability to translate self-awareness into behavior change is essential to a successful career. Few experiences are more satisfying or more critical to building confidence and self-esteem than developing a new skill or giving up a bad habit when we know we should. Conversely, repeated experiences of trying and failing to change behavior leads to what psychologists call learned helplessness, which leads to a victimized, vulnerable, and resentful orientation toward one's career and life over time.

In the unpredictable and rapidly changing global workplace, you must be prepared to adapt or risk being left behind. Adapting is nothing more than a combination of giving up old habits and learning and mastering new ones. The twenty-first century self-empowerment skills—listening (for feedback), self-discipline, and self-directed learning—provide the foundation for self-directed behavior change. However, even with that foundation, achieving long-term behavior change is very difficult.

How many New Year's resolutions did you stick to versus give up on? How many times did you promise yourself to never lose your temper again, to stop saying yes when you mean no, or to give up smoking, only to go right back to the old habits? Being aware that a habit is counterproductive is often not enough to prompt change. In extreme cases, realizing that if you do not change your behavior you might die—as in smoking—may not be enough to get a person to change.

On the other hand, the idea that people do not change—"We are who we are"—is patently false. All human beings develop skills and change habits over the course of their lives. Even if it takes you five failed attempts to stop smoking before you stop for good, the bottom line is that you changed a habit.

People develop new skills and behaviors either because they have to or because they choose to. For a change you *have to* make (to survive), the environment and circumstances provide the motivation necessary to get past the inconveniences, anxiety, and discomfort that long-term habit change involves. For change *you choose to make*, the motivation and determination must come from you. Self-directed behavior change is much more challenging and far more prone to failure. Knowing what to expect on the road to change and being able to anticipate those points along the way where you are most likely to derail can give you a real advantage.

THE ROAD TO BEHAVIOR CHANGE

We know that habit change is never easy. The following graph illustrates the temorary dip in comfort and effectiveness that occurs from the time you discover the negative impact of a long-standing habit until you reach the point when the new behavior becomes automatic.

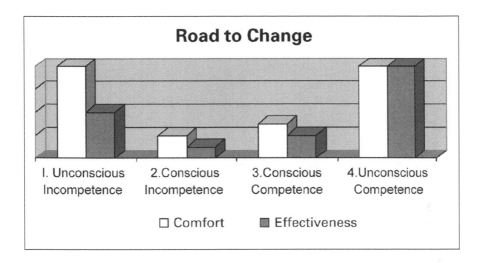

In the Comfort Zone

Phase 1. Unconscious Incompetence

You are unaware of those aspects of your behavior that are counterproductive.

Frank's sarcasm was described as "part of his charm" by friends who knew him well, but to his work team, his sarcasm was experienced as insulting and demeaning. It was so ingrained in his style that he was largely unaware of it. Frank was in the "Ignorance is bliss" phase of development: What you don't know about yourself can't hurt you. It was only after feedback from his wife in marriage counseling and from his boss in explaining why he was passed over for a promotion that Frank veered out of his comfort zone and into conscious incompetence.

Outside the Comfort Zone

Phase 2. Conscious Incompetence

You become aware of the counterproductive behaviors and feel uncomfortably self-conscious and awkward.

Frank went from carefree, natural, and self-assured in how he interacted to constantly self-doubting and worrying about hurting other people's feelings. Not exactly sure how he was coming across, his self-censoring was making him feel vulnerable and ineffective. With no outlet for communicating his disagreement, he was extremely frustrated. Had it not been for his wife and supervisor's insistence that he work on disagreeing more respectfully, he would have quickly lapsed back into his old habits. As Frank became more aware of the critical and non-accepting thoughts and feelings that preceded his cutting reactions, he began to understand which phrases were particularly problematic for colleagues (e.g., "Yeah, right," "Try again," and "Another brilliant idea") and to learn techniques for disagreeing in an agreeable way, he moved to the third phase of behavior change, which is conscious competence.

Outside the Comfort Zone

Phase 3. Conscious Competence

You become conscious of the things you can do to be effective, but incorporating them makes you feel self-conscious and uncomfortable.

In this phase, Frank developed a menu of tools and techniques he could apply from reading a self-help book, guidance from the marriage counselor and his manager, a workshop, and observing people he respected. He spent time writing scripts for what he might say instead of being sarcastic, practicing with friends, and gradually applying these new techniques in real-life situations with colleagues. At first, there was no doubt that his efforts to tone it down felt forced and awkward. But he did begin to notice a more open and friendly quality to these interactions, which motivated him to continue to work on his communication and get past the robotic phase and into the phase where his new, more adaptive habits start to become automatic. When that happens, Frank is in Phase 4: Unconscious Competence.

In the Comfort Zone

Phase 4. Unconscious Competence

The new skills finally become unconscious or habitual, and you are effective and comfortable.

Being aware of the challenges you will face in changing your behavior is only one of the keys to successful long-term change. In the following section you will find recommendations to ensure successful long-term behavior change.

THE KEYS TO SUCCESSFUL BEHAVIOR CHANGE

Select one or two behaviors to tackle at a time. One of the biggest mistakes people make is taking on more than they can manage. Even something as simple as becoming a more effective listener is likely to require a tremendous amount of sustained focus to achieve.

Be absolutely certain that you are ready to commit. Successful habit change comes long after we realize that a habit is counter-productive. There needs to be enough evidence from the feedback you get that (a) links specific behavior with the negative impact, (b) specifies how your behavior is hurtful or counterproductive to others or yourself, and (c) shows that if you don't change you will not be able to achieve results that are very important to you or you will risk losing someone or something that is very important to you. In the case of listening, reminding yourself of the bigger prize, and therefore avoiding derailment, provides internal motivation. In much the way substance abusers usually don't change until they hit rock bottom, habit change does not occur until lots of negative feedback directly tied to that behavior makes us reach a tipping point. While you might become aware of many things to do more or less of as you read this book, probably just a few habits are ripe for the changing.

Do not wait for your workplace culture to support and reinforce habit change you are ready to make. The fact is that most habit change occurs with the organizational current in your face. For example, Andrea has committed to becoming more inclusive, while her boss and her boss's boss manage autocratically. James is working on being more appreciative in spite of the fact that the last two promotions in his departement were for people who almost never offer praise.

Make sure the behavior you want to change is specific. "Being a better listener," "exercising more," or "being more positive" are all very broad concepts that are made up of a number of specific behaviors and habits. For example, "allowing other people to finish their thoughts" is one of several habit changes that will lead to being a more effective listener. (If you go to the Listening Habits Self-Assessment on page 90, you will find several other such habits.) Focusing on each habit separately is the way to go.

Recognize that you have a choice in every decision you make. When you tell yourself that you no longer have to respond to people in your usual way just because that is the way you have been responding for many years, you have come a long way toward effecting change.

Let others know what you are trying to achieve. Not only will making your development goals public add to your incentive to persevere, but it is likely to motivate others to be more supportive.

Work from a realistic, structured development plan that clearly defines your goals, the steps necessary to get there, and a means of gathering feedback along the way. Development Planning forms can be found on pages 176–180.

It is natural to respond to the frustrating moments in learning a new skill by judging and putting yourself down. Much of the time we are not even aware of how unaccepting and intolerant we can become of healthy, necessary mistakes. Failure is a necessary part of success. If you are not failing, you are not stretching. Adopting an accepting, supportive, and compassionate attitude toward yourself is critical to sustaining the motivation and enthusiasm necessary to achieve your development goal. The collateral payoff is becoming more aware and in more control of how you treat yourself.

1. Write down two habit changes you successfully made (e.g., quitting a bad habit such as smoking, starting or sustaining a healthy habit or lifestyle change).

_____

_____

_____

_____

_____

   a. What was the hardest part of making that change?

_____

_____

_____

_____

   b. To what do you attribute your success?

_____

_____

_____

_____

2. Think of two lifestyle or habit changes you were not able to successfully make.

_____

_____

_____

_____

_____

   a. To what do you attribute your failure to make the change?

_____

_____

_____

_____

_____

CHAPTER 15

NETWORKING

Tom Friedman's description of the highly globalized or "flat world" in which we live underscores just how critical developing a strong network is to career success:

> Around the year 2000 we entered a whole new [globalized] era . . . the thing that gives it its unique character is the newfound power for individuals to collaborate and compete globally . . . individuals must and can ask "where do I fit into the global competition and opportunities of the day and how can I, on my own, collaborate with others globally?"[17]

If you are not connected through a global network of relationships, you may as well be working in a cave. Building a strong network as early in your career as possible gives you a distinct competitive advantage because of the following:

- **Networking maximizes your value added.** Unlike technical, analytical, and customer service roles, which are those most likely to be outsourced, networking skills that give you access to key industry players make you indispensable.

- **Networking gives you true career mobility.** It is the best way of finding a job. By some estimates, more than 70 percent of all jobs are filled through informal networking channels. Even when you have a good job, a strong network is critical to remaining abreast of global trends and opportunities you may wish or need to take advantage of at any given time. Your network allows for career mobility and freedom of choice so that the many job and company changes you are likely to make over your lifetime will be made with you in the driver's seat. The information you get from your network will help you to understand your world from an external perspective and make you more aware of critical market trends, what is going on in the job market, what skills are most in demand, and what jobs are most and least vulnerable to outsourcing. All of this information is critical to managing and optimizing your market value. Your network empowers you to come and go on your terms.

- **Networking sharpens your influencing skills.** The communication and relationship skills you develop as you build your network will serve you well throughout your career. Just as speeches, debates, and interviews with media hone the influencing skills of politicians, the networking process hones your influencing effectiveness. Through networking, you learn how to market and promote yourself, meet new people, and listen.

That being said, most people feel uncomfortable networking and avoid it like the plague.* The following comments from clients over the years reflect some of the more common biases: "I hate promoting myself," "It feels dishonest and insincere," "I am not good at small talk," "I don't like to be seen as asking for handouts," "It's a waste of time," "No tangible results," "Shy people can't network," and "Outgoing people are great at networking. My work speaks for itself."

---

* Ironically, some of the most talented early career "stars" often neglect building networks and honing their networking skills because job opportunities and advancement come easily as they start their careers. At mid-career, they risk reaching their limit if they have not learned how to develop a network.

The key to successful networking is approaching it with Connecting Style in mind—yours and the style of the person with whom you are networking. The Connecting Style model can help you to identify the natural networking strengths, weaknesses, and strategies that are most effective for you. Knowing the Connecting Style of the person with whom you want to network will help you tailor your approach to build a stronger, more satisfying connection with them. (Refer to Chapter 8: Guidelines for Connecting with Each Style.)

The next few pages contain valuable networking advice gleaned from workshops in which each style group discussed their networking experiences and lessons learned.

First, let's meet four individuals each representing a Connecting Style at the welcoming cocktail hour at a pharmaceutical industry offsite. Charlie (Analytical) is a model networker, and yet he is hardly a schmoozer. Charlie discussed the industry's latest technology innovations with one person over the course of the hour, whereas Carl (Energizer), also a strong networker, engaged a dozen colleagues with his interesting and often entertaining stories. Although June (Supportive) interacted with more people than Charlie but far fewer than Carl, she ended the evening knowing a lot more about others (owing to her excellent listening skills) than they knew about the important work she has been doing (owing to her modesty). Debbie (Driver), who showed up late because she was finishing a critical conference call with her team back at the office, interacted with a number of people. Unlike Carl, Debbie did not seek out others as much as others initiated contact with her. Preoccupied with reports waiting to be reviewed back at her hotel room, Debbie left at the earliest opportunity, having felt she wasted valuable time.

ANALYTICALS

Strengths: Charlie, like many Analyticals, builds highly effective networks around his interests. Analyticals are likely to be very active in churches, communities, politics, and professional associations, where they form deep friendships with people who share their interests. Charlie is the president of his state chemical engineering association, a school board member, a member of a traveling brass band, and active contributor to a number of community and political committees. At work, he is typically on a number of task forces inside and outside of his department. Those relationships, while task- and interest-centered, are enduring and deeply rooted in mutual respect, a common set of values, and a shared experience of accomplishment and contribution.

In task-focused settings like those mentioned above, many of the personal qualities that characterize the less forcefully assertive styles blossom, contributing to their networking success. Analyticals and Supportives step up as fine, confident leaders and mentors when dealing with subjects they understand and in which they take an interest. Finally, the reliability and long-term commitment characteristic of Analyticals contribute to building trust that makes others comfortable sharing even the most sensitive information with them.

Challenges: Analyticals find networking to be a challenge when it moves away from building relationships around mutual interests to building relationships to serve their own interests, such as networking with the intent of finding a job or selling a product or service. For Analyticals, it goes against their independence and professional pride to ask for help—they would much prefer to help others. In addition, Analyticals' strong sense of fair play makes them feel like networking to advance one's career is a form of cheating and degrades their professional standards.

SUPPORTIVES

Strengths: The advantage for Supportives when it comes to building a network comes from building on their strengths as team players. They are natural relationship builders and perhaps the most engaging and engageable type. Therefore, like Analyticals, a great road to building a strong network is joining organizations, associations, and committees representing causes or subjects that matter to them. As members, they slowly build strong relationships based on the contributions they make and the support they provide. They volunteer generously, can be excellent listeners and great team players in supporting roles, and have little trouble fitting in. The overall impact is quite positive in supporting others' needs to feel understood, included, respected, and valued. Supportives can build the kind of networks that give them tremendous access based on the mutual trust and loyalty they typically cultivate with others.

Challenges: The hard part for Supportives is breaking through the resistance of joining new organizations to begin with, and who can blame them? Unlike Analyticals, who are often quite confident in the technical expertise and abilities they offer committees and organizations, Supportives can be much less self-confident and fear being rejected or seen as not as good as others. Supportives place more importance than Analyticals do on how welcoming an organization is. Supportives often find it much more comfortable to join new organizations with friends or colleagues.

More than any other style, Supportives are extremely uncomfortable with the self-promotional aspect of networking. They prefer to support and help others and avoid the spotlight. That being said, networking provides a great opportunity for Supportives to factually describe the value they add, the qualities they bring to an organization, and the track record that reflects those qualities. This exercise often forces the supportive to get past their fear that raising expectations will lead to their disappointing people. Through networking, they get to practice the arts of requesting help, marketing their accomplishments, meeting new people, and otherwise establishing a professional presence among colleagues—all examples of assertiveness that also will bolster their effectiveness in their personal lives.

ENERGIZERS

Strengths: Energizers fit the image of what most people imagine when they think of a great networker. They are quite gregarious and welcome the opportunity to meet and socialize with all types of people in all types of situations—people they have never met or old friends. They approach social situations with confidence and warmth and know how to fit in and put others at ease. They are natural promoters and spend a good deal of time sharing and selling their ideas. Like Charlie, Carl volunteers on many committees, attends conferences, and is active in his community.

Challenges: Energizers make a strong impression—usually a very positive one. However, if they do not balance their talking with listening and awareness of others' Connecting Style, they risk making an unforgettable negative impression. A strong network is built up over time and requires a level of consistency, commitment, and dependability that are not strengths for many Energizers. They can be very passionate, connected, and committed one day and move on to something else more exciting the next. They have a very strong need to feel understood, valued, included, and respected and can be quite sensitive to rejection. Therefore, relationships can sour more easily based on perceived slights. Although Energizers appear socially bold, it is not uncommon for them to build networks almost exclusively around nonthreatening people—those who they feel look up to them, while avoiding those who they consider a threat.

DRIVERS

Strengths: When they do meet people, Drivers, like Debbie, make a very favorable impression. Unlike Energizers, Drivers don't worry too much about pleasing people, so they tend to be very direct, to the point, and confident. They build instant credibility as they come across as extremely results-oriented and competent—just the kind of strong performer with whom colleagues want to be associated. Their potential as network builders is limited only by their motivation to invest time and energy.

Challenges: As much as Drivers can build strong networks, very often they don't, especially outside the world they live in every day. They tend to be so overbooked (since the organizations they work for become very dependent upon them) that they don't have time for networking. Drivers will pursue networking to the extent that they can see a direct and tangible benefit to the success of their organization or the work they do.

Like Analyticals, the fierce independence of many Drivers makes them uncomfortable asking for help from others, including when they are looking for a job. Once they recognize how critical networking is to a successful outcome, they discipline themselves and go about building a network. After they find a job, or no longer see an immediate need to network, their networking activities can drop off precipitously. As with Energizers, Drivers need to learn that networking depends on long-term and consistent contact with their network. Over time, the lack of a strong network can hurt them in that it limits not only their field of vision of their industries but also their own marketability.

RECOMMENDATIONS APPLICABLE TO ALL FOUR STYLES

1. Build on your strengths by being active in as many organizations that represent your interests as you can. Select an association and join it.

2. Enroll in a public speaking workshop or training program as soon as you can. These experiences are perfect for people from all four Connecting Styles. They seem to be quite effective in building influencing skills and bolstering confidence in a structured, safe, and enjoyable setting. The organized and goal-oriented approach, the opportunity to see that most people are as uncomfortable as you are in selling themselves, and the feedback and highly participative nature of these programs contribute to making it a very positive experience. The hard part is getting yourself to sign up.

3. Building a network is a direct function of paying attention to and responding to the Six Basic Connecting Needs. Review the behaviors in Chapter 3. Notice how applicable all those behaviors are to building a strong network.

4. Block out one hour per week on your calendar and devote this time to building and refreshing your network.

CHAPTER 16

STRESS RESILIENCE

"I have learned that success is to be measured not so much by the position that one has reached in life as by the obstacles which he has overcome while trying to succeed."

—BOOKER T. WASHINGTON, SCIENTIST (1856–1915)

Human beings are, as individuals, highly flawed works in progress. Put us together, and in spite of the best intentions, we will inevitably bang into each other and step on each other's toes. While this is largely unintentional, there is no limit to the collateral aggravation we each give and get to one degree or another every time we go to work. With all of the difficult personalities, politics, mutual mistrust, and dysfunctional leaders, the workplace is a fertile field in which to cultivate patience and resilience. Your performance will be judged, in part, by how well you can keep the assorted frustrations from undermining your motivation and great work.

THE GREATEST STRESS TRIGGERS

By far, the greatest stress triggers are people who "push our buttons." While explosive arguments and nasty interactions may be most memorable, traumatizing, and damaging to a relationship, the interactions that take the biggest toll emotionally and physically (i.e., headaches, stomach problems, anxiety, depression, sleepless nights, irritability, eating disorders, obsessive rumination) are the daily insults and violations we quietly endure and feel powerless to change.

The fact that most stress is interpersonal in nature is just as true for task-oriented Drivers and Analyticals as for relationship-oriented Energizers and Supportives. While style is predictive of the kinds of people and habits that are most disturbing, people across all styles and cultures know how stressful it is to work around people who, unknowingly, make you feel criticized, marginalized, ignored, misunderstood, used, deceived, violated, exploited, manipulated, undermined, controlled, excluded, treated unfairly, or otherwise disrespected. It can be rather depressing when we discover that the other person seems totally unreceptive to feedback or working it out. Worse still is when we can't avoid the offender because our roles are so interconnected that we have to see them every day. Worst of all is when the source of our torture is someone with the authority to control our compensation, assignments, and job security (the boss).

The distress we feel inside is merely triggered by what other people say and do to us. These are the lemons life gives us. How toxic they are to our system has a lot to do with how we process and respond to them. Some people are born with thick skin and the ability to slough off almost anything. Others—in particular those who are more relationship-oriented, empathetic, and naturally trusting—have to work harder to protect themselves from the destructive impact of working closely with toxic people. If I may mix metaphors, this chapter provides you with the insights and tools for making lemonade out of lemons.

MY HOTTEST HOT BUTTONS

Nearly twenty years ago, a client mentioned that of all the insights he gained from the many stress-management workshops he attended, the most valuable was that "stress is the difference between expectation and reality." And after twenty years, I have seen just how many of the most effective stress-management tools and practices are based on that principle. If we manage our expectations based on *what is* rather than on what *we wish* it to be, we are much less likely to feel frustrated, angry, or disappointed. In that spirit, the first line of defense against getting stressed out is identifying the behaviors most likely to elicit an overreaction in you—commonly referred to as "hot buttons."

THE HOTTEST HOT BUTTONS

The *Hottest Hot Buttons* exercise will help you identify those commonplace frustrations, humiliations, and denigrations most likely to get under your skin. Once identified, you can focus on inoculating yourself from these habits by following the stress resilience tips presented later in this chapter.

Directions: Rate how irritating you find each of the behaviors listed below by placing an X under the appropriate number in the columns to the right. **1 is the least irritating and 5 is a major irritation.** When you are done, enter the three most irritating behaviors in the table following, and refer to the instructions there.

My Hot Buttons	How Much It Irritates Me				
	1	2	3	4	5
1. Being asked to do work that you consider beneath you					
2. Seeing supervisors or peers bending or breaking rules without consequences					

My Hot Buttons	How Much It Irritates Me				
	1	2	3	4	5
3. Having work you are proud of casually dismissed					
4. Discovering that your supervisor assigned your task to someone else as well					
5. Discovering you made a mistake					
6. Presenting to an unknown or unreceptive audience					
7. Making a request of your supervisor					
8. Being criticized					
9. Being rejected					
10. Being confronted					
11. People who require constant attention					
12. Being manipulated					
13. Dealing with people who can't make up their mind					
14. Being talked down to					
15. Serious people who never express their feelings					
16. Being micromanaged					
17. Having to stand up for yourself					
18. Dealing with unreliable people					
19. Being excluded or dealing with cliques					
20. Seeing people get undeserved recognition					
21. Being constantly interrupted					

After reading the entire chapter, draft a development plan to inoculate yourself from overreacting to your hottest hot buttons (use the forms on pages 176–180). Over the coming months, rate your irritation after thirty, sixty, and ninety days.

My Three Hottest Hot Buttons	30 days	60 days	90 days
1.			
2.			
3.			

Any of these stressors have the potential to make you feel threatened and activate your survival response—commonly referred to as fight or flight, which means exactly what it sounds like. When confronted with danger, you will either stand and fight or beat a hasty retreat to safety. Once useful to protect us from hungry saber-toothed tigers, this outdated survival mechanism shuts down the most evolved regions of the brain where relationship and communication skills reside and activates the most primitive regions. Unable to distinguish between psychological and physical threat, we overreact to stress across the board and find that our rational thinking has been emotionally hijacked.

Fight-or-flight is:

1. Automatic and constantly adjusting in response to perceived threats

2. Physical
   - Cardiovascular
   - Neurological
   - Muscular
   - Digestive
   - Dermatological

3. Emotional
   - Hurt
   - Defensive
   - Impulsive
   - Angry
   - Scared

4. Mental
   - Capacity to process important information blocked
   - Difficulty interpreting others' behaviors and intentions
   - Impaired judgment
   - Inflexibility

FIGHT-OR-FLIGHT IMPACT ON BEHAVIOR BY CONNECTING STYLE

The distinguishing characteristics of each style intensify under stress, and as the judgment centers become dulled and our resources feed the fight-or-flight engines, the behaviors we count on as assets can become liabilities.

ANALYTICALS	SUPPORTIVES
Go from *critical thinker* to *detached* and	Move from *team player* to *enabler* and
• remove themselves emotionally.	• make excuses for others to minimize tension.
• become difficult to engage.	• have trouble asking for what they need.

DRIVERS	ENERGIZERS
Move from *director* to *dictator* and	Move from *passionate team leader* to *overpersonalizing* and
• take over.	• attack.
• bulldoze and exclude.	• blame and criticize.

GETTING YOURSELF OUT OF FIGHT-OR-FLIGHT

When you feel on the verge of going into fight-or-flight, pause until you regain your emotional balance. Once you calm your mind, you can *respond* based on a more balanced and complete understanding rather than *react* impulsively. Bad things happen to good people when they react immediately after being challenged, attacked, or insulted. The more wronged you feel, the more important it is to drain your brain of fight-or-flight hormones before taking action. Your emotionally hijacked brain will urge you to disconnect from your vulnerable feelings by fighting back or withdrawing. Your pride shoves your best judgment aside and wants to run things, making you likely to say things that seem appropriate at the time but may prove regrettable. Even if you can find the right words, when in fight-or-flight mode your body language is likely to broadcast your emotions and cause confusion and defensiveness. An angry or defensive tone can have a powerful and lasting negative impact on the other people in the room and undermine your credibility and ability to influence.

Deactivate fight-or-flight with deep breathing or any relaxation or meditation technique that works for you. For example:

> *Begin to focus all of your attention on your breathing. If you open your mouth slightly, you will notice a cool sensation on your lips, which will relax you and be a good focal point.*
>
> *As you inhale, locate and stay aware of your physical fight-or-flight symptoms—such as the knot in your stomach, dry mouth, or a tight lower back. As you exhale, breathe out the discomfort. Staying connected with the vulnerable feelings and embracing the negative experience as a learning moment keeps you from acting, opens the door for increasing self-awareness, and makes you more receptive to working out the issues. More often than not, you will discover a different, more balanced perspective on the stressful situation, leading the way to a more constructive approach.*

It's Not Personal: Let go of insisting that other people treat you the way you think you deserve to be treated. The way people behave toward you says more about them than you.

The Mighty Pause

"We desire to be happy and at peace, but when our emotions are aroused, somehow the methods we use to achieve this happiness only make us more miserable."[18]

Reacting to a frustrating or provocative situation or person when the fight-or-flight hormones are still coursing through your brain is like driving when drunk. Not only do you pose a danger to yourself and others, but also the judgment and impulse control required to refrain from engaging the wheel or person is also impaired. Even if you are lucky enough to avoid disaster, at the very least, you can be assured that whatever point you wanted to get across will be lost, as your emotional overreaction becomes the center of attention. It's a lose-lose.

When you find yourself in fight-or-flight and are about to act, which for most humans (but especially *Energizers and Drivers*) is likely to be several times a day—the simple act of pausing can interrupt your reaction before it takes shape. A three-second pause, especially when accompanied by a deep breath is accessible to us at even the highest levels of emotional arousal, and creates enough of a gap to allow us to get back to present moment where we can:

- Notice what's happening from different perspectives—especially that of the object of our frustration.

- Pay attention to the thoughts, emotions, and physical feelings happening "now."

- Consider other ways of understanding the situation that might be less personally threatening.

- Become aware of what you really want (besides hurting another person or proving you are right), and whether your planned reaction is going to get you there.

Pausing can even open us to our hearts and allow our emotional intelligence, natural kindness, and compassion to influence our response.

Try pausing for a few seconds and taking a deep breath right now. What was that like for you?

If this is something you want to incorporate, try using the pause button at least once today at even the slightest hint of frustration or stress, and see where it takes you. As a reminder, try hanging the word "Pause" on the fridge or wherever else you are likely to see it.

GETTING SOMEONE ELSE OUT OF FIGHT-OR-FLIGHT

When you are interacting with someone, regardless of style, who is in fight-or-flight mode, it is pointless and self-defeating to argue, explain, debate, or tell him or her to calm down. The only productive response is to help the person get out of the fight-or-flight spiral. Here's how:

- Listen, listen, and listen. (Nonjudgmentally with acceptance.)

- Restate what you hear. ("So what I hear you saying is . . .")

- Reflect the person's feelings/emotions. ("I hear how frustrating this is for you. . . .")

- Ask clarifying questions designed to get the person to express his or her emotions in words. ("Would it be okay if I ask a question? What exactly is so frustrating about this?")

- Try to figure out which of the person's needs have been violated. This will help you to figure out how to deal with the stressor. ("Hmmm, it sounds like she was not consulted before the decision was made and probably feels excluded. . . .")

Once the person calms down, you can move on to addressing the problem or issue at hand.

If you know the Connecting Style of the person you are trying to calm down, you may wish to incorporate these additional factors into the way you approach them:

Drivers: Once you notice a driver taking over, the only effective response is to be direct, but not overly emotional or personal. If they notice that you are beating around the bush or sulking, they will deliberately ignore you.

Energizers: Energizers respond well to feeling understood and listened to. Although it can be quite challenging to keep from joining the argument or pushing back, that would be a mistake. Allow them to unwind and stay engaged but calm and the anger will burn itself off.

Analyticals: Once you notice that an Analytical has withdrawn and disengaged out of frustration, give them their space and some time before approaching them about what they are reacting to. When you do, let them know in a calm tone that you are interested in understanding what's on their mind and if they are ready, they will open up. But be prepared to hear their perceptions spelled out directly and often harshly. Simply getting it off their chest may not do. If they feel they are owed an apology, they will wait for it and be ready to move on once they hear it.

Supportives: When Supportives get quiet in response to their buttons getting pushed, a supportive response works best. They appreciate the interest shown in them and the opportunity to express their frustration or make a request about how they wish to be treated. Unlike Analyticals, they are open to being approached as soon as you notice. They don't need to be given time and space, nor do they care about apologies. They are eager to feel understood and to be reassured that they have not hurt anybody or caused others to have a negative opinion of them.

MANAGING FIGHT-OR-FLIGHT IN GROUP SETTINGS

One of the first management roles you will experience is leading a meeting, focusing a discussion, or presenting to a group of colleagues. You are now responsible for facilitating the activity and, to some degree, managing other people's behavior. This is a role that forces you to assert yourself and risk hurting others' feelings (Drivers and Energizers, beware) or not asserting yourself and risk being and feeling taken advantage of (Analyticals and Supportives, beware). In addition to applying the behaviors that support the Six Basic Connecting Needs, you can use some "stress-tested" phrases to address some of the common challenges you will face as a manager. Being prepared with the right words can make a big difference in your confidence and effectiveness. Practice these silently or aloud, imagining in detail the scenario that applies to each. In time, you will get a feel for what works best for you.

Challenge	Constructive Approach
Responding to a chatterbox who won't shut up at your meeting	Stop speaking and say: • "I'd like to have everyone's attention so you all hear what is being discussed." • "It seems like there are a number of conversations going on. So that we get everyone's valuable input, may I please ask that we have one conversation at a time? Thank you."
Disagreeing with someone	First, make sure you understand the other person's point of view. Then take any of the following approaches: • Say, "Yes, and . . ." adding your point of view. • "I appreciate your perspective and would like to add . . ." adding your point of view. • "I hear what you're saying, but I see it differently . . ." adding your point of view.
Getting someone to stop dominating a conversation at a meeting you are leading	Using a firm tone and moderate voice, say: • "Thank you for all your input; I would like to see what others have to say." • "Thank you for all your input; let's see what others have to say." • "You have a lot to say on this topic, John. To make sure others can also voice their opinions, let's give them a chance to speak now." • "To ensure we have everyone's input, I'd like to use the next few minutes to hear from those who have not yet had a chance to speak."
Drawing out others who have not provided input/feedback or voiced their opinion	While looking around the room, particularly at those who have not yet spoken, say: • "We've heard a lot of great ideas so far. How about hearing from those who have not yet spoken—even if it's to say that you agree or disagree with what's been said so far."

Challenge	Constructive Approach
Getting an off-topic conversation back on topic	Offer the following thoughts: • "That sounds like a great idea, and I want to allow enough time to explore it fully, so why don't we add it to the agenda of our next meeting (or discuss it in private)?" • "We seem to have gotten off on a tangent, so I'm going to bring us back to the agenda. Did you want to continue that conversation offline or add it to the agenda of our next meeting (or explore it further and report back to the group in out next meeting or . . .)?"
Handling someone who constantly interrupts the conversation	Using a firm tone and moderate voice, say: • "So we can hear everyone's complete thoughts, may I suggest that when someone is talking we let them finish their statement, give people a moment to think about what was said, and then respond?"
Getting your voice heard	Sit upright and lean into the conversation; maintain good eye contact; use a firm tone and clearly project your voice when you say: • "I would like to add . . ." • "I agree, and . . ." • "Perhaps we should consider . . ." • "Yes, and . . ."

THE SECRET TO STRESS RESILIENCE

Certain people seem to constantly be overwhelmed by stressors while others facing the same adversity are able to take it more in stride. We call this stress resilience. What differentiates these people are coping skills that serve to keep things in perspective, reinforce a sense of being in control rather than being controlled as a victim of circumstances, and keep them from taking things too personally. The following section describes the qualities that stress-resilient people share in common.

STRESS RESILIENCE SELF-ASSESSMENT

The following habits and characteristics differentiate those resilient people who are truly able to manage highly stressful work situations from those who get sick, angry, depressed, or otherwise stressed out. This exercise allows you to determine how prepared you are for pressure and to identify specific areas to help increase resilience.

Directions for Scoring: Rate yourself on how often you demonstrate each of the following stress-resilient habits by placing an X in the appropriate box (Often, Sometimes, Rarely). Count the number of X's in each column and enter the total number in line 19. Multiply the number in line 19 by the number in line 20. Enter the result in line 21. Add the three scores together from line 21 and enter the total in line 22. Refer to the key at the bottom to determine your level of stress resilience.

Stress Resilient Habits	Often (1)	Sometimes (2)	Rarely (3)
1. I can accept the things I cannot control.			
2. I set my expectations based on reality rather than insist that reality conform to my expectations.			

Stress Resilient Habits	Often (1)	Sometimes (2)	Rarely (3)
3. I have few rules for how the world should behave.			
4. I see obstacles, adversity, and even failure as challenges to overcome and opportunities for growth.			
5. I know how to make lemonade out of lemons.			
6. I don't take it personally when my basic needs are ignored or violated by others. I do feel hurt, angry, and the like, but I know how to get past those feelings and solve the real problem.			
7. I have a strong network of support and am not afraid to call on that network for help rather than carry burdens alone.			
8. Rather than respond as a victim waiting to be rescued, I take action to solve my own problems.			
9. I effectively manage my time with good planning and preparing in advance.			
10. I try to keep my long-term career goals in mind so that short-term frustration does not bother me so much.			
11. I accept the fact there will always be detractors. I don't let other people's opinions of me define who I am.			
12. I strive for personal excellence, but I can set limits and say no to requests from my boss that I can't fit on my plate.			
13. When I feel someone is taking advantage of me, I can assert myself before I boil over.			

Stress Resilient Habits	Often (1)	Sometimes (2)	Rarely (3)
14. I can let things go and forgive others and myself.			
15. I measure my success more in terms of what I contribute to others than what I get for myself.			
16. I maintain a healthy work-life balance.			
17. I can live in the here and now rather than bemoan the past and worry about the future.			
18. I don't take myself too seriously. I can laugh at myself.			
Subtotal			
Multiplier	x1	x2	x3
Score for Column			
TOTAL SCORE			

KEY

Score	Stress Resilience
18–24	Very Resilient
25–34	Resilient
35–42	Borderline Stress Risk
43–54	Stress Risk

PART FOUR

Connecting at Work

CHAPTER 17

STYLES AT WORK

The examples in this chapter illustrate how the Six Basic Connecting Needs and Connecting Style can be applied to significantly enhance your personal effectiveness. Note that in each of these interactions, disconnects related to style differences between well-intentioned people can quickly become highly emotional, personal, and destructive conflicts that undermine relationships and impact business results.

A SUPPORTIVE AND ANALYTICAL IN CONFLICT

When Nat first joined the department, Mark, his supervisor, was very friendly and supportive. Their group was in a small open area where four people worked in close proximity. When Nat's father got sick, Mark went out of his way to support him by accommodating his schedule, driving him places when necessary, and generally making himself available. Yet as much as he appreciated Mark's support, Nat began to feel uncomfortable. His need for privacy and space grew, and his stress level mounted in relation to Mark's increasing univnited efforts to help and support him. He began spending more time away from his desk, and when he was in the common work area, he was less socially responsive.

Mark took this personally. He felt unappreciated and hurt and made the mistake of raising the issue as a work-related concern by insisting that Nat act more friendly (for the benefit of office morale) and that he let Mark know where he was at all times "in case customers called asking for him," all of which seemed bogus and highly offensive to Nat's need for privacy. Nat, in turn, became even more remote and outright irritated with Mark. Once things had escalated, their personal dynamics seemed to reverse: Mark went from going out of his way to make life as comfortable for Nat as possible to making him quite uncomfortable.

Mark, a Supportive, started out by treating Nat the way he would like to have been treated if he were in the same situation—with warmth, support, and increased availability. Nat, an Analytical, valued privacy and control and simply needed some space. The harder Mark tried, the more Nat needed to pull away. As Nat picked up resentment from Mark, he felt threatened and even more remote.

The Lesson

What went wrong?

1. Lack of understanding each other's Connecting Style and how to connect based on style

2. Assuming bad intentions when the other felt treated in a way that made him uncomfortable

3. Being unresponsive to the following key connecting needs:
   - Nat's need to feel understood, respected, empowered (allowing him to feel in control), included, and trusted
   - Mark's need to feel valued, included, and understood

How could this have been avoided?

☑ If Mark had asked Nat how he could be most helpful at this difficult time, it might have supported Nat's needs.

☑ If Nat had expressed appreciation for Mark's extending himself, it might have met Mark's needs and would have helped him relax.

Drivers: The Hard Road from Loner to Leader

Making the transition from an individual technical contributor to manager can be difficult. A new manager must redefine personal and professional effectiveness to include not only technical excellence but also the ability to motivate, assess, develop, and influence people individually and collectively. Some of the most technically gifted and individually effective managers have had their careers sidelined indefinitely by their inability to collaborate. People with such qualities as competitiveness, independence, aggression, dominance, and the need for control—some of the very traits traditionally associated with individual corporate success—seem especially vulnerable.

There is evidence that when the Driver's competitive behavior exceeds a certain level of aggression, performance gets worse for the Driver as an individual, their teammates, and the team as a whole as teamwork breaks down.*

Roger, a Driver with Analytical secondary style, was an engineer in a consumer products company. He was assigned to be a project manager less than a year out of school. He had a reputation for hard work, unmatched business knowledge, unflinching competitiveness, and a quick, intuitive, steel-trap mind.

Roger usually worked independently or with a small team of like-style peers. His accomplishments had earned him a reputation as someone who could get things done. With his highly competitive and aggressive style, he soon became a favorite of the boss, clearing the way for a fast trek up the ladder to manager within a few short years out of school.

But Roger was developing a reputation for being "impossible to work with." As far as he was concerned, there was his way and the wrong way. He was a black-and-white thinker who hid his

---

* Study of undergraduates playing a flight simulation game requiring teamwork to win, showed that too many aggressive teammates leads to weaker performance and breakdown of team playing across all members. M. C. Bowler, D. J. Woehr, J. R. Rentsch, & J. L. Bowler. (2010). "The Impact of Aggressive Individuals on Team Training," *Personality and Individual Differences, 49,* 88–94.

vulnerabilities behind a mask of total self-reliance, confidence, and control. He was available to those who needed his help, but he showed little patience for opinions, approaches, or work styles that differed from his own.

Ironically, Roger's colleagues saw the competitive, aggressive style for which Roger had been so well rewarded as insensitivity, defensiveness, and overcontrol. His intimidating style compelled others to feign agreement with him or avoid him. That pattern, along with his tendency to surround himself with like-style individuals as his closest subordinates, enabled Roger to maintain an unrealistically positive view of himself as a project manager. In the meantime, he had created a highly repressive atmosphere in which most team members felt devalued and underutilized.

In time, disaffection and turnover increased among his staff as did complaints to the human resource manager. Morale was low, as were loyalty, creativity, and innovation.

Encouraged by his human resources manager, Roger began to practice a more participatory style of management. For example, he tried delegating more responsibility to subordinates, but he was too anxious about giving up control to allow his people to take approaches different from the ones he preferred. Rather than truly allowing autonomy, he continued to rescue, control, and second-guess people on his team—in effect, undermining their confidence and authority. This pressure brought out the worst in his people and reinforced his excuse for not being more participative: "They are not ready for it."

The Lesson

Over the next four years, Roger was passed up several times for promotions and transferred laterally to other areas. Then the roof caved in. A peer steadfastly refused to work with him, and his mentor retired.

Roger was read the riot act: "We value you, need you, and want you, but your career now depends on your ability to work effectively with others. People-handling skills are now the bottom line."

With the help of an executive coach, Roger made good progress in the developmental objectives judged critical to his success (improved skills in listening, conflict resolution, assertion, and consensus building). He became more sharply aware of his blind spots and the effect of his behavior on others. His personality did not change dramatically, but he was able to modify enough of the dysfunctional behaviors to make a difference in his effectiveness.

Energizers: Listen to Your Audience

Energizers are known as visionaries with a natural ability to inspire, motivate, and engage others. Just as Energizers' strengths can be larger than life, so can their blind spots. As I learned during one of my earliest consulting assignments, when Energizers become too passionate about their ideas, they risk losing touch with their audience and engagement turns into disaffection.

Rose (Energizer) was a charismatic sales manager who asked me to help her understand why her sales force (largely service-oriented Supportives) was failing to sell a new, highly profitable investment product to their customers. From her perspective, this was a product they had requested, and one she went out on a limb to get funded.

As is typical of Energizers, Rose's response to the poor results was blaming and attacking. "They are the ones who asked for this. They couldn't wait to get it. Are these the right salespeople? Maybe we should replace a few with stronger people."

Extensive interviewing revealed a major disconnect. Rose's salespeople did not believe in this product from the start. Trained to be customer-focused, they had lots of doubts about how beneficial it would be, despite its profitability to their firm. It is true that Rose heard a lot of enthusiasm, but the apparent buy-in was mostly a function of people's perception that she was in love with the strategy, she had already made up her mind, and disagreeing with her would be hazardous to their continued employment. And yet Rose was incredulous to learn that her employees had not openly shared their differences with her. "I told my people a thousand times that my door is always open and I want honest feedback."

Taking her up on her wish to be perfectly honest, I suggested that while she thought her sales force was totally onboard with this product, their desire to please her kept them from sharing their deep concerns and objections. I also shared with her my doubts that replacing staff would solve the problem.

The Lesson

The more powerful an Energizer's passion, the harder they have to work at getting people to share their independent opinions. Recall that the keys to influence include supporting others' needs to feel understood, included, appreciated, respected, and empowered. In this case, none of these needs were supported, and the connection between Rose and her sales team never happened. This would have been the case across all styles, but it is especially true of Supportives. Apart from being self-protective, Supportives are reluctant to burst other people's bubbles. If they have doubts about what they hear from an Energizer, they are just as likely to dismiss their doubts as trust them. Rose needed to work hard to get genuine buy-in. She would have had a much easier time of it had she allowed the sales force to be involved in creating the new product. Supportives need to take more risks in giving voice to their opinions and doubts. Their naturally nonthreatening style and sensitivity to others' pride makes their voice the easiest for Energizers to hear. Still, Supportives should expect a defensive reaction at first and not let it discourage them from asserting their opinions.

As if to confirm the accuracy of my findings and the instincts of her sales force, Rose thanked me for my excellent assessment and promptly replaced me with a consultant who was smart enough to agree with her. By the way, the fact that I am also an Energizer may have contributed to her difficulty digesting my findings. If I had to do it again, I would have spent a lot more time asking her questions and allowing her to give voice to her frustrations prior to sharing a report.

CHAPTER 18

ENTRY: CONNECTING TO THE ORGANIZATION

"Fools rush in where angels fear to tread."

—ALEXANDER POPE, "ESSAY ON CRITICISM" (1709)

It's hard to imagine better guidance for effectively entering an organization than that offered to coauthor Greg Mortenson in the internationally bestselling memoir *Three Cups of Tea: One Man's Mission to Promote Peace . . . One School at a Time*. Summarizing what he learned from the wise elder Haij Ali about how to elicit cooperation from rural Afghani communities, to which he planned to donate and build desperately needed schools, he writes:

> Haji Ali spoke. "If you want to thrive in Baltistan, you must respect our ways. The first time you share tea with a Balti, you are a stranger. The second time you take tea, you are an honored guest. The third time you share a cup of tea, you become family, and for our family, we are prepared to do anything, even die. Doctor Greg, you must take time to share three cups of tea. We may be uneducated but we are not stupid. We have lived and survived here for a long time." That day, Haji Ali taught me the most important lesson I've ever learned in my life. We Americans think you have to accomplish everything quickly. . . . Haji Ali taught me to share three

cups of tea, to slow down and make building relationships as important as building projects. He taught me that I had more to learn from the people I work with than I could ever hope to teach them.[19]

And although Mortenson refers specifically to underdeveloped societies that have existed for hundreds of years, these principles apply to gaining acceptance in any new community or group. Let's look more specifically at how they apply in the modern workplace.

LAYING THE GROUNDWORK FOR SUCCESS THROUGH RELATIONSHIP BUILDING

The most leverage you will ever have in your career is during the first thirty days in a new organization—the phase referred to as "entry." I would love to see it renamed "engagement" so that people understood immediately that it represents the beginning of a relationship rather than a territorial intrusion. As I see it, way too many qualified people get tripped up during entry because they try to do too much too soon, without the benefit of a solid connection with the world they are attempting to impact.

Entry represents a narrow window of opportunity to lay the groundwork for future success. The first and hardest step to realizing this opportunity is simply acknowledging what may appear to be two contradictory ideas at once. You are the right person for the job, and you can't succeed in the job until you understand the organizational and human context of the goals and objectives with which you are charged. Your new organization's culture and values, the subculture of your department, the personalities and politics all create a gravitational pull on you and everybody who lives in or interacts with it. The more aware you are of these forces, the better you can control and leverage them. Ignore them, and they will control you. Starting off in discovery sends a very respectful message that goes a long way to gaining the trust of your new colleagues as well.

For Drivers and Energizers the stress of entry may make you more impulsive and action-oriented, putting you at risk for unknowingly confusing, intimidating, or offending people. Resist the temptation to act, remind yourself that much of what you think you know is probably wrong, and instead access your ignorance to jump-start the process of soaking up everything around you like a sponge. The more you can empty your mind of all presumed knowledge and assumptions based on past successes ("the fog of success"), the more your brain will want to fill itself up again with new information.

However, the experience of ignorance can be very uncomfortable to many otherwise strong performers. The thought that "I understand all I need to understand to act" gives us a welcome sense of control and competence. Confusion, ignorance, and cluelessness make some people feel so dependent, incompetent, and out of control that they can't tolerate "I don't know," even if temporary and appropriate. The reality is this: *Ignorance is temporary and leads to competence. Arrogance is permanent and locks out the learning that leads to competence.*

Turning ignorance into competence requires time to walk around, explore, research, and engage people. The entry phase should allow ample time for this. If you find others pulling you into activities that deprive you of this exploration time, most people will understand and agree to your postponing of nonurgent activities to allow room for learning. For most people, the biggest challenge is fighting off their own urge to get involved too soon in too many things.

While Analyticals and Supportives are more careful to gather information before making a decision, they often know a lot more than they give themselves credit for and can be too reluctant to press forward with their ideas. When you feel overwhelmed by how little you know in comparison to others, you need to ask, "What are all the things I do know about the challenges facing me?" You might be surprised at all the valuable insights you've gained simply by all the quiet listening and observing you do.

When joining a new team, some people are at greater risk of being too confident and acting on solutions before accessing their ignorance (ready, fire, aim). Others are lacking in confidence and wait too long before expressing and acting on solutions (ready, aim, aim).

1. In the following space, describe your natural approach to entry, including your strengths, weaknesses, and hot buttons.

_____

_____

_____

_____

2. Once you have written down your self-perceptions, ask one or two others who have observed you during on-boarding to share their perceptions of your on-boarding strengths, weaknesses, and hot buttons. Jot down the main themes and the implications for how you can be more effective.

_____

_____

_____

_____

WHAT YOU SEE IS NOT ALWAYS WHAT YOU GET

First impressions can be as revealing as they are deceiving. Keep in mind that your initial presence will provoke "stranger anxiety" in the existing population. Stranger anxiety is a defensive reaction that temporarily heightens people's awareness of and cautiousness around strangers. Even though you don't feel like a stranger, to new people that's what you are—and until they get to know you, you're perceived as a threat. Nothing personal. You may know how good your intentions are or how much you have to offer. But this innately programmed response does not recognize intentions. You have to prove your trustworthiness with actions.

Stranger anxiety manifests itself differently according to style. Supportives and Energizers may become uncharacteristically welcoming, attentive, and protective in response to an unknown newcomer. They genuinely want to help them, but this approach also protects them by building a bond with the newcomer and adding them to their list of allies, thereby increasing their probability of survival. Biologically determined reactions sound manipulative when describing their function, but the person who behaves this way is genuinely motivated to be helpful and generous.

Analyticals and Drivers respond to strangers by being uncharacteristically guarded and reluctant to engage until the new person proves his or her worthiness. This behavior can be experienced as rejecting or insulting and can form long-standing resentment from the new person if it is taken personally. If you can accept that the initial response you get from others when you step foot in their territory is not directed toward you, but toward their survival, you stand a good chance of taking it all in with patience, tolerance, and acceptance.

It might make it easier to tolerate this initial testing of your patience if you put yourself in their shoes. You made a decision to enter this new community. Most of the people you meet will have had no input into your joining their world. This makes them more skeptical and less motivated to make you successful. You also had lots of time to prepare mentally for your arrival. They have not. And finally, any change in an organization will be perceived as increasing the chances of success and survival for some and as a threat to survival for others. And you have no idea who fits into which category.

Describe your typical reaction to people as they join an organization, group, or team of which you are a longtime member?

_____

_____

_____

_____

_____

The reception you get is also influenced by the organization's culture and climate. Sometimes, the reception you experience has a consistent flavor across all the people you meet and is either positive (warm and welcoming) or negative (cool and unwelcoming). When the feeling you get is based on attitudes that pervade the organization, it is telling you something important about the culture and climate of the organization. For example, if you feel welcomed and supported, existing employees are probably made to feel valued and included by management and are likely to be receptive to what you have to offer fairly shortly after your arrival. On the other hand, if you feel invisible, avoided, and devalued, don't take it personally because it is most likely a symptom of a dysfunctional culture in which little trust exists among employees, or of a situation in which people feel vulnerable, as with a recent or impending layoff, poor business performance, an investigation, or any number of destabilizing events. In the event that the organization is in a precarious place, your job is to stay friendly, not overreact, and activate your curiosity to understand what is going on and its impact on individuals with whom you work.

THE RULES FOR SUCCESSFUL ENTRY ARE UNIVERSAL AND TIMELESS.

Entry rules apply to entering a new school, neighborhood, club, or team and are probably hardwired by evolution into our nervous systems. Humans are territorial and, subsequently, very sensitive to who belongs and who doesn't. When a stranger appears on the scene, all current occupants within a space focus their attention on trying to answer one very Darwinian question: *"Is this stranger's presence going to increase or decrease my chances of surviving? Is she/he a friend or foe?"* Almost all of the do's and don'ts for successful entry relate to convincing people that you "come in peace."

1. Enter with humility, respect, and admiration.

2. Enter as an "anthropologist" whose purpose is to understand the culture and people, not as a "missionary" whose purpose is to convert and civilize others based on your values and point of view.

3. When you notice that the "emperor has no clothes," chances are everybody already knows it, so there is no need to say it.

4. Demonstrate that you are willing to play any role asked of you (within reason) without complaint.

5. Show others that you are willing to learn and play by the rules.

6. Be very careful not to criticize, lecture, complain, or badmouth others. Find a good sounding board outside the organization for the first few months.

7. Stay neutral in social situations. There are many people who feel victimized and are eager to share their negativity with new people. "Hey, Steve, don't expect any appreciation from Sally (boss)."

8. Don't talk about how much better your former organization was.

9. Ask, "How can I help?" rather than assume that people automatically want your help just because you believe you can be helpful.

Although these rules seem to be common sense, most people find them very hard to follow. The most frequently cited derailer for new employees at all levels is entering as a change agent, or "missionary," before understanding the lay of the land, rules, culture, people, and priorities and establishing the connections that lead to being empowered by employees to make an impact. Whatever good intentions might be motivating you to launch a change effort immediately upon arrival, you are implicitly criticizing the people who were there when you arrived—the very people needed to help you implement the change. Musician Jimmy Cliff said it best in the song "The Harder They Come": "The harder they come, the harder they fall, one and all."

It's not difficult to understand why newly recruited people bypass commonsense rules and look to make a difference the second they enter the situation. The recruiting and hiring process leaves the candidate with:

- A bias toward action rather than assessment (new candidates may already feel they understand their mandate and the challenges from the interviewing process).

- The need to live up to the lofty expectations they created during countless hours of interviews spent convincing senior executives that "If hired, I will exceed expectations, be a transformative leader, save money, increase efficiencies, pull a rabbit out of my hat, and turn water into wine."

- The hiring and senior executive's perspective on the priorities, problems, and challenges (which is a very narrow and incomplete slice of the full picture).

- The mistaken belief that being hired by a senior executive or even the CEO automatically translates to the authority to lead.

Your success and impact as a leader and change agent depend on getting blessed and empowered by the people with whom you work—peers, partners, and followers. You already established a connection with those involved in the hiring process—your focus from day one should be identifying, engaging, and connecting with everyone else within your sphere of influence.

Created by the forces of human nature, organizational cultures are much like ocean riptides. Hidden beneath an inviting surf just offshore, a riptide pulls everything out to sea, even while the waves above roll in toward the shore. No man or woman, no matter how strong a swimmer, stands a chance swimming against the riptide. But an average swimmer who understands and respects its laws can easily get to shore by swimming with the riptide for a short while, then parallel to shore, and once out of the riptide, swimming into shore.

Chris's Unfortunate Entry

Although Chris was hired as a senior executive in a "dysfunctional" organization, the lessons learned from his experience apply to anyone entering a new organization.

A very bright, enthusiastic, and technically strong Driver-Energizer, Chris was hired to integrate the multiple technologies from different retail businesses that were acquired or merged under one company. If there was a common theme echoed by business and operational executives during his multiple interviews, it was the urgency of realizing the functional advantages and cost savings of an integrated-technology platform.

The frustration conveyed by nearly every executive from the corporate floor due to the failure of people from the different business units to cooperate thus far was palpable. The successful candidate was someone who had successfully implemented a similar large-scale technology solution and demonstrated the ability to bring people together and transform a resistant culture of easily threatened people with big egos who sabotage each other.

After many hours of interviews, Chris convinced the "executive collective" that he was the man for the job. But the interviews also left Chris with the burden of entering the new job with a residue of their biases, collective frustration, and devaluing attitude toward the people with whom he would be partnering and leading to get the job done.

Chris soon discovered countless problems with cost overruns, useless meetings, poor attitudes, and unqualified or poorly trained employees. The totality of his experience thus far, combined with his natural take-charge style, led to a short-circuiting of his discovery and engagement phase and an entry approach that caused people to feel ignored and excluded.

By the time Chris discovered for himself that the challenges were much more complicated than good-guy corporate executive leaders thwarted by bad-guy business unit leaders and change-resistant legacy employees, he had already alienated himself from so many key people that his incumbency never got off the ground. By the way, he discovered that senior leadership was as resistant to change as any constituency. Had Chris entered with an open mind, ready to engage people where they were and genuinely listen, understand, value, respect, include, and empower them, he would have been in a much better place to eventually lead.

AN EFFECTIVE APPROACH TO ENTRY

The following approach to entry is far more effective and true to the principles described in the Six Basic Conncting Needs:

1. *Activating your curiosity* and making people feel understood, appreciated, respected, included (useful and helpful to you), and empowered. This discovery process is a big part of what leads to engagement. If existing employees feel that a new employee is judging them and their organization, they will close down and undermine that individual. By keeping a focus on understanding and appreciating, employees will feel trusting, understood, valued, respected, include, and empowered, leading to their support of the new employee.

2. *Deactivating* your urge to form conclusions, criticize, and rescue.

3. *Assessing* which problems are urgent and need addressing, and addressing them right away (in a way that engages others).

A mutually understood performance agreement settled prior to the start helps the new employee to arrive at the right balance of doing, learning, and engaging and keep on track. The most significant obstacle to entry success is ambiguity around expectations. Candidates' excitement about what a great opportunity they are about to realize brings an equally powerful anxiety about what they stand to lose if they ask too many questions or make requests. This is a universal experience, so expect to feel a very strong urge to push the offer through without delay, and then deal with any confusion afterward. The problem is that once you agree to an ambiguously defined role, you have very little leverage to make the necessary changes or clarifications in your agreement.

So while your heart wants to just get the offer and begin the work, before you start, you must discipline yourself to negotiate a mutually understood performance agreement with clear roles, responsibilities, and success measures. This applies regardless of role and rank. In the long run, it's a win-win for you, your boss, your organization, and your customers.

The On-Boarding Checklist in Appendix C will help guide you through that expectation-setting process.

CHAPTER 19

LEVERAGING CONNECTING STYLE DIVERSITY

"No man is an island, entire of itself;
every man is a piece of the continent,
a part of the main."

—JOHN DONNE, ENGLISH CLERGYMAN AND POET (1572–1631)

So far, we've applied the Connecting Styles model to enhancing your individual effectiveness in relationship building. But Connecting Style awareness is also critical to optimizing your effectiveness as a problem solver, innovator, and decision maker. The fact is that since any one style represents just one of four different perspectives and problem-solving approaches, surrounding yourself with and incorporating the thinking and perspectives of individuals from the other three styles gives you a distinct performance advantage, and there is a significant body of research backing this up.

The autobiography of Paul Allen, co-founder of Microsoft, provides a great example of just how advantageous diversity can be:

> The main reason the tandem held together for more than
> a couple of years was that each of the entrepreneurs brought
> something valuable to the table. Mr. Gates's single-minded
> focus on winning everything, whether a chess game or a vital

business deal, was complemented by his partner's ability to see the bigger picture—an ability reinforced by Mr. Allen's eclectic set of outside interests, ranging from music to sports to science fiction. Mr. Allen acknowledges that the two men were "extraordinary partners." He likens their union to that of Bill Hewlett and David Packard, or Larry Page and Sergey Brin, the founders of Google.[20]

Yet no matter how convincing the research may be, it is no match for the powerful human instinct to seek out those most like us, and fear and avoid those least like us. The fact is that most teams lack the diversity advantage because they are either made up of people who think similarly or, among those teams that have a diverse makeup, inter-style tensions lead to people competing rather than leveraging each other's perspectives. In the case of Paul Allen and Bill Gates, the conflicts between their styles led them to split up, which resulted in Paul Allen leaving Microsoft in 1983.

This chapter will make you more aware of the advantages of style diversity and the dire consequences of style imbalance (group-think), and help you overcome biases that may keep you from tapping into style synergy. In addition, it makes suggestions for dealing with the tensions working across styles can bring.

THE POWER OF DIVERSITY

We owe our very existence to diversity. Diversity is what enables a species to survive and adapt in the face of extreme threat and adversity. The species that survives a ravaging virus does so because of the variation in immunities among its population. The species that survives a new and dangerous predator does so because some run really fast, others swim really well or fly really high, and some just taste really awful.

The recent research of Scott E. Page (University of Michigan) offers empirical evidence in support of the competitive advantage of organizational diversity:

> Mathematical models demonstrate that diverse groups of problem solvers outperformed the groups of the best individuals . . . diverse boards of directors make better decisions, and the most innovative companies are diverse.[21]

Scott's research shows that when the members of a group have a diverse set of mental tools:

> Group decision-making is less likely to get stuck at suboptimal solutions, and more likely to arrive at superior ways of doing things. Roughly, given certain initial conditions, if we take two populations, one in which cognitively all agents are above average and another that is random and diverse, the latter regularly will out-perform the former in solving problems.[22]

So why are truly diverse teams and organizations so few and far between? Most leaders already think their team or organization is diverse. Token representation enables non-diverse decision makers to make all the key decisions without regret. And the more successful a team, the more its leaders seek to replicate what they already do, the less they feel they need to learn, and the more they resist outside influence.

In fact, forced integration of people from diverse style groups onto the same team causes initial defensiveness, tension, and antagonism that actually lead to diminished performance in the beginning. Some of the more common universal reactions that serve to make diverse team building a challenge when someone different is initially introduced are:

- The need to be right

- The need to feel invulnerable

- The need for order and control

- The aversion to confusion and ambiguity

- The attraction to simple solutions

- An aversion to the unknown

- Suspicion of people, ideas, and styles that are different

- The tendency to discount, devalue, and reject what we don't understand

Making the team greater than the sum of its parts, or leveraging the collective IQ of a diverse group, is a process. It requires strong leadership, time, and the opportunity for people to understand each other, become aware of their biases, learn to tap into each other's complementary assets, and appreciate each other. Eventually, inclusiveness becomes a habit across all dimensions, and the more people develop the habit, the more it becomes part of the organizational style. Until then, a mandate for diversity gently introduced may be necessary to insure that people have ample exposure to this productive team experience.

GROUPTHINK

A diverse team is only as strong as those least empowered to contribute and make an impact. It is quite common for people to feel pressured to support the majority and censor their own potentially provocative ideas in order to survive. This is commonly referred to as groupthink.

The term *groupthink* was first used in 1952 by William White in *Fortune* magazine to describe faulty group decision-making caused by an autocratic team culture that rewards conformity and discourages disagreement.[23] The most extreme example would be the 1986 disaster of the space shuttle *Challenger* when, according to *NBC News* space analyst James Oberg, "Engineers who had qualms about the O-rings were bullied or bamboozled into acquiescence."[24]

In some cases, like the *Challenger* disaster, pressure to conform is observable and even openly discussed and acknowledged inside the organization. *But in most cases, groupthink overtakes healthy debate unnoticed.* Most people are unaware of contributing to or being part of groupthink. It's like a Trojan Horse that becomes apparent only by looking back at a disastrous decision that seemed sensible at the time.

In referring to the decisions leading up to the 2007 banking crisis, Nobel Prize–winning economist Paul Krugman asked in a September 2009 *New York Times* article, "How Did Economists Get It So Wrong?"[25] What he describes is essentially a faulty decision-making process caused by overrepresentation of Analyticals. The disastrous decision to deregulate markets was based on the shared but faulty consensus of the economics profession who, as stated by Krugman:

> "went astray because economists, as a group, mistook beauty, clad in impressive-looking mathematics, for truth. They fell "in love with the old, idealized vision of an economy in which rational individuals interact in perfect markets."[26]

When any workgroup, no matter how brilliant, is dominated by one Connecting Style and confuses its collective truth with "The" truth, it is at high risk of failing. In this case the truth, as defined by these Analyticals, was an assumption that markets would respond predictably based on mathematical models, and human decisions would be driven by rationality and reason. Krugman's observation is a great example of the insidious but clear impact of style imbalance:

> Unfortunately, this romanticized and sanitized vision of the economy led most economists to ignore all the things that can go wrong. They turned a blind eye to the limitations of human rationality that often lead to bubbles and busts; to the problems of institutions that run amok; to the imperfections of markets—especially financial markets—that can cause the economy's operating system to undergo sudden, unpredictable crashes; and to the dangers created when regulators don't believe in regulation.[27]

It's not surprising, based on what the Connecting Style model teaches us, why this picture of reality included everything in the Analyticals' comfort zone: a rational, predictable, and neat world best expressed through mathematical models. Everything they missed just happens to be what they are least comfortable dealing with—messy, emotional, irrational, and unpredictable realities, and "all aspects of the truth that, if they understood them, would have resulted in recommendations to regulate markets. Decisions that would have resulted in a very different outcome for the world economy," said Krugman.[28]

Energizers feel very comfortable with, and much more likely to identify and understand, the messy, ambiguous, emotional, and irrational realities that Analyticals and, to some extent, Drivers don't readily process. But the folks whose perspective of reality would have been most valuable to the economics profession also happen to occupy the quadrant opposite Analyticals. The habits and qualities that most irritate Analyticals are essentially the defining characteristics of the Energizer, which may explain why the two realities never found each other. The people who are most critical to successful decisions are likely to be those whose styles are most frustrating and annoying for most of the people in a workgroup! The more diversity, the greater the risk of conflict. But even with that conflict, the benefits outweigh the risks.

Lurie's Groupthink Recipe

1. Take a workgroup of well-meaning, talented people who share similar background and style.

2. Place in an organization with a world-class brand in an uncertain and volatile market.

3. Bake under pressure to deliver short-term results.

4. Remove job security and, voilà!—Groupthink!

Warning: Style diversity will keep groupthink from gelling.

Eight Groupthink Symptoms

Yale University research psychologist Irving Janus clarified our understanding of the nature and influence of the groupthink process and the organizational conditions in which it is most likely to grow and thrive. Janus identified eight symptoms most characteristic of groupthinking teams, which are listed and defined below. Given the disasterous consequences and enormous costs that groupthink decisions can have, the more time you invest in familiarizing yourself with this list, the less time it will take to recognize and hopefully address this scourge.

1. *Illusions of invulnerability*

2. *Rationalizing warnings* that challenge the group's assumptions

3. *Unquestioned belief* in the morality of the group

4. *Stereotyping* and attacking those who are opposed to the group

5. *Direct pressure* to conform by equating dissent with disloyalty

6. *Self-censorship* of ideas that challenge consensus

7. *Illusions of unanimity*—silence is viewed as agreement

8. *Mindguards*—self-appointed group members who shield the group from dissenting information[29]

CHAPTER 20

STAYING GROUNDED

"Don't follow leaders, watch your parking meter."

—Bob Dylan, "Subterranean Homesick Blues,"
Bringing It All Back Home

A toast to your career success, from a familiar Irish blessing:

May the road rise up to meet you.

May the wind be at your back.

May the sun shine warm upon your face and the rains fall soft upon your fields.

And to ensure that you are fully protected:

May you always be treated fairly.

May team players who do all the hard work and play by the rules be recognized and rewarded.

And may those who live by their own rules and care only about themselves suffer the consequences.

May you never be pressured to agree when you really disagree.

May you never have to compliment an emperor on their clothing when they are wearing none.

*And may you never have to conform with self-serving leaders
who abuse their authority and put profits and power ahead of
principle and people.*

But just in case wishing doesn't make it so:

*May this chapter help prepare you to deal with the working
world as it is—namely, highly imperfect, sometimes unfair,
and unpredictably frustrating.*

In today's economy it seems that "Cheat or be cheated" and
"Everyman for himself" are quickly becoming acceptable options
to "Work hard," "Play by the rules," and "Team first" as the defining mottos in many American industries.

ADVERSITY AND THREAT

*Whether threat and adversity are more likely to bring out the best or worst
in you is highly situational. But you always have a choice.*

Just as adversity and threat can cause survival instincts to kick
in, bring out the best in us collectively and individually, and lead
to accomplishment once thought unimaginable, it can also lead
to an "every-person-for-oneself," "win-by-any-means-necessary"
response that brings long-term disastrous consequences.

For example, the intensity of competing in the Olympics
and the Tour de France has propelled some athletes to world-
record-shattering performances, and others to illegal, performance-
enhancing drugs.* In the corporate world, market pressures have
led to the innovation of new technology, products, and services
that contribute real value to real people, just as they have led to
increasingly exploitive strategies that manipulate companies' loyal
customer base to purchase homes, investments, goods, and services

---

* Facts have come out since I originally wrote this section that require moving
Lance Armstrong from the category of world-shattering record breaker to that
of liar and cheater.

they don't need or that are outright harmful, and with money they don't have.

While highly unscrupulous characters come out of the wood-work and certainly prod and profit during these times, it's mostly honest, hard-working, well-intentioned people who, out of the instinct to survive, keep lowering their ethical bar to adapt to eco-nomic realities while rationalizing their behavior with the every-one-else-is-doing-it principle. This standard seems to define the ethical code of conduct of our times: Cheating and stealing, lying, throwing people under the bus, and so on are wrong *unless people do it in sufficient numbers that it becomes a competitive disadvantage not to do so.* The groundwork for cheating and the-means-justifies-the-ends thinking starts in high school if not earlier.

As the pressure to get outstanding grades and to get into a good college has increased, so has the frequency of cheating. The 2009 Josephson Survey of 29,760 high school students found that 64 per-cent of all students have cheated at least once and 38 percent more than twice. Yet 93 percent of those surveyed were satisfied with their personal ethics and character.[30]

Michael Josephson, who through his institute has been studying cheating in a variety of settings for several years, makes the con-nection between the normalization of cheating and the recent near-collapse of the global economy. "What is the social cost of that [cheating]—not to mention the implication for the next generation of mortgage brokers? In a society drenched with cynicism, young people can look at it and say, 'Why shouldn't we? Everyone else does it.'"[31]

Cheating and other forms of corruption have increased in the workplace as well. The 2009 PricewaterhouseCooper, LLP survey on corporate crime reported that as economic conditions worsen, "a growing number of executives, it seems, are discovering that the only way that they can hit their performance targets is to break the law."[32,33]

The survey also found that just 26 percent of executives reported economic crime in their organizations, compared with 34 percent of respondents from lower ranks: a disturbing pattern given that those with the most impact on shaping culture appear to be more accepting of criminal behavior.

It's hard to deter this behavior when many executives go unpunished or even profit in spite of these crimes, which is more than can be said of the countless victims of defective and/or deadly foods, feeds, medicines, automobiles, military supplies, and aeronautical, mining, drilling and environmental safety systems (to name a few of the business crimes reported in the media this year).

Although most of you would like to believe that you would find a way to resist participating in shady practices, especially when they have real victims, the famous experiments that social psychologist Stanley Milgram conducted on obedience to authority figures, and subsequent research validating those findings suggest otherwise:

> I set up a simple experiment at Yale University to test how much pain an ordinary citizen would inflict on another person simply because he was ordered to by an experimental scientist. Stark authority was pitted against the subjects' [participants'] strongest moral imperatives against hurting others, and, with the subjects' [participants'] ears ringing with the screams of the victims, authority won more often than not. The extreme willingness of adults to go to almost any lengths on the command of an authority constitutes the chief finding of the study and the fact most urgently demanding explanation.
>
> Ordinary people, simply doing their jobs, and without any particular hostility on their part, can become agents in a terrible destructive process. Moreover, even when the destructive effects of their work become patently clear, and they are asked to carry out actions incompatible with fundamental standards of morality, relatively few people have the resources needed to resist authority.[34]

Being aware of how integrity can be compromised is an important means of avoiding getting sucked in. There aren't identifiable villains you can avoid. Rather, it is a very insidious process in which borderline behavior taking place around you slowly chips away at your sense of what is and isn't acceptable. For the entry-level employee, you may be exposed to behavior that ever so slightly crosses the line without consequence from the moment you enter a new organization, including:

- Taking credit for work others have done

- Claiming time you did not work, stealing office supplies, exaggerating expense reports

- Exaggerating resumés and accomplishments

- Sneaking a peek at and sharing confidential information

- Unfairly blaming or denigrating colleagues

- Manipulating the system to get the best assignments and perks

- Manipulating the boss to earn his or her favor

When senior leaders model this behavior and seem to reward some of the worst offenders with raises and promotions, it is understandable how some might conclude that these behaviors are all "necessary to playing the game." But once you start setting your ethical bar based on the lowest common denominator, it's like digging a hole you are standing in: You lose the perspective and the leverage you need to get out of it.

INOCULATING YOURSELF FROM CORRUPTING INFLUENCES

Conforming to the culture and behavioral norms of your workplace, and trusting and following your leaders, are necessary in order to become a trusted and influential part of that community. But so is retaining your independent thinking and judgment. Sometimes it's best to compliment the emperor on his handsome outfit, and sometimes you have to let him know he is not wearing any clothing at all.

You will have to draw the line by using your judgment, situation by situation, in a way that is true to your core values. To make your boss successful in the long run, sometimes you will have to say and do things that are likely to make him or her feel frustrated with you in the short term. Differences of opinion and perspective are only valuable if they are communicated. Sometimes, leaving an organization is the best choice.

These represent some of the most difficult decisions you will have to make. While you can't avoid them, there are ways to stay grounded enough to keep from losing your balance altogether, and making good decisions consistent with your long-term goals and core beliefs.

THE 10 KEYS TO STAYING GROUNDED

1. *Understand your rights* and company ethics policies and procedures.

2. *Foster self-awareness.* Knowing who you are, your core values, what is important to you, where you are going, and what you want to leave behind enable you to:

   - Feel less dependent on approval, admiration, status, and material trappings. "Money is great, but I want to build, create, deliver, serve, help . . ."
   - Be more tolerant of everyday barriers and frustrations.

3. *Focus on career mobility.* Cultivate a current network, marketable skills, a track record, and job-search skills.

4. The *willingness to acknowledge "trouble"*—in organizations and individuals—is the first step in your sprint away or disengaging from it.

5. *Long-term goals* tied to contributing to a greater good make you much less vulnerable to corruption, whereas goals that have to do with getting as much as you can for yourself make you more vulnerable.

6. The support of *a strong family, community, and network* of social support is something you can tap into when you feel unsure of a decision or begin to question yourself.

7. Identify *mentors* you can trust and turn to when faced with difficult choices.

8. Have a *well-rounded life and outside interests* to give you a balanced view of the world and who you are in it.

9. Exhibit *wisdom and courage* to do the right thing, even when no one is watching.

10. Accrue enough *savings* to allow you to make changes without causing major financial disruption!

Finally, let me leave you with this wish from the 2008 movie *The Curious Case of Benjamin Button*:

> "Be whoever you want to be. There is no time limit. Start whenever you want. You can change or stay the same. There are no rules to this thing. You can make the best or the worst of it. I hope you make the best of it. . . . I hope you meet people with a different point of view. I hope you live a life you're proud of. And if you find that you're not, I hope you have the strength to start all over again."

Appendices

PREPARING OUR TEENS FOR CAREER SUCCESS

For those of you whose children will soon be entering or have recently entered the workplace, this appendix lays out a parenting approach based on the Connect for Success principles. (Incidentally, the Connecting Styles model and tools are fully incorporated into *Handbook for Early Career Success*, available at LEDONLINE.com.)

Our young men and women go off to their first jobs with diploma in hand, hopes high, and raring to go. Congratulations, by the way. That is a huge accomplishment for them and you. What they don't have is a rulebook for workplace success or the experience and wisdom to easily navigate the workplace at first. With fewer children and more time to parent (and worry), giving them advice based on our experience is almost irresistible. We want to prepare them for the challenges they will be facing—to be there for them just as we always have. But during this phase, the need to define their own identity and prove their independence can make them more defensive to direct advice from Mom and Dad.

Besides, giving advice to young adults is a delicate challenge for which many of us feel unprepared and unsure. The very power of our hopes, dreams, and fears for our sons and daughters makes it hard to be objective and raises questions like: "When do I share my opinions about what is best and how?" "How involved should

I get in helping them to choose what they want?" "How do I get them to be more responsible?" "When is my advice useful, and when is it unwanted or experienced as overbearing or critical?" Great questions! So let me suggest some guiding principles you can apply to making these decisions on your own and to making the most of your role as a parent during this phase.

PARENTS HAVE A SUBSTANTIAL ROLE TO PLAY

While this is true, it should be more of a supporting role, which is successfully played by being quick to encourage and listen, slow to rescue and advise, and careful never to criticize and judge. It's all about enabling and empowering your son or daughter to tap into their own strengths and resources in responding to the challenges of entering the unfamiliar and often overwhelming world of adult-hood. And although you may be less actively involved in their lives, their strength and confidence is derived from the sense of trust you show in them by not overreacting and intervening. Some teens are harder to connect with during this phase than others. This is a very transitional phase of life, and young men and women try on different roles, feel intense emotions, and are likely to blow off steam at the people they feel safest with—their parents. So become as attuned as you can to what is going on with your children, with your own feelings, fears, worries, and moods. Allow your feelings and thoughts, but be very careful not to react to what your mind is telling you. A lot of the anxiety parents experience about their child's success is fueled by concerns about getting older, facing an empty nest, and the anticipated loss of the most prominent position in their lives.

The most common questions parents ask me are related to how they can get their children to be more receptive to good parental advice. We want to prevail upon our child to make the decisions we think are best—about the schools, friends, and classes they choose; about how to behave; the habits to break and develop; and so on. This is all part of the coaching function of a parent. Yet by the time a child reaches adolescence, they will accept only so much coaching from us. As they grow from late teens to early twenties, they are reaching the moment in their lives when they are as smart as they will ever be and we are as dumb as we will ever be. In other words, just at the time they are moving into their careers, our role as giver of wisdom is quite limited. So don't keep pushing against a locked door. It will only frustrate you and cause you to feel resentful toward your sons and daughters.

The reality is that life is the best teacher. People are most open to learning when they are in a situation that challenges them in a way that makes clear that what they already know doesn't get the result, and it cannot be ignored because it hurts or deprives them of some great opportunity.

1. *Listen.* Children learn the most from those with whom they feel safe sharing their most difficult experiences when they are feeling most vulnerable. We want one of the people they seek out to be us! For this reason, honing and activating nonjudgmental listening-for-understanding skills constitute the most important priority. Effective parenting at this stage is all about listening loudly and advising quietly and selectively. It is about connecting with your children in a way that gives them the good feelings that will encourage them to keep you in the loop and share more and more honestly what they are struggling with at a given moment. Our children will be able to figure out for themselves most of the problems they face on the job, or they will identify peers and mentors with the right expertise to help them (an important collaboration skill that will grow as we pull back). Rarely do they need direct advice as much as they need to vent, think things through, get validation and support, and feel a connection with a strong family support system to which they can turn whenever they need it.

2. *Help them to see the best in themselves.* Our job as parents is mostly to keep our children confident enough to keep trying, even when they feel like giving up. The more quickly we instruct, the more

they are reminded that we will step in, and the less likely the chance they will discover and access their own resources. Achievement is rarely about talent, knowledge, and skills. Rather, it is about optimizing what we have, and that requires pushing the envelope and taking chances, and being willing to fail on the way to success. The path to success is always through adversity. So let's not deprive them of that by giving solutions prematurely.

3. *Manage your own worries and fears so your children's job doesn't become protecting you from worry.* Our kids have a way of sensing when we are anxious and worried about them. They then respond by taking care of and protecting Mom and Dad by telling them what they want to hear. Our protective parental instincts make it very hard to be objective about our children. We tend to worry too much and underestimate our child's ability to find their own successes. It is important to be aware of when you might be communicating your worries and fears about their future to them. Remember that as real as they may seem, your anxieties and fears about your child are just thoughts—thoughts driven as much by your own history and psychology.

4. *It is very important to help our grown children take risks with us, encourage them to push back, and let us know when we are being helpful and less than helpful.* Then we need to respond to their feedback in a way that encourages them to give us more.

To achieve this, we must be prepared to feel frustrated, useless, and helpless. Their struggles stimulate our parenting instincts, and we have to get used to the frustration of not being able to comfort them. Like the lessons learned the first time we drop them off at kindergarten, they can't begin to grow until we separate from them.

Raising independent children requires a more or less continuous stream of letting go so they can leave us and then come back as stronger and more developed human beings. It means living with the immediate risks attached to flying out of the nest for the first time to face the world at their most vulnerable, and there is no escaping those trials and tribulations. Calluses don't grow on feet that never touch the ground, and self-confidence cannot develop without being on one's own to sink or swim and live with the consequences.

TWO FINAL THOUGHTS TO KEEP IN MIND

1. As much as we think we teach our children by what we say, we all know that what they learn from us is what they see us do and how they experience us day in and day out. Who we are is who we are, and that is what we give them.

2. As life goes on, they will have increasingly more access to people with subject matter expertise that matches their needs at that time, freeing us up to fulfill the role we do best: being moms and dads and the number-one source of the unconditional love upon which they rely.

DEVELOPMENT PLANNING FORMS

Directions for Creating Development Plans

1. Write your development goal. Be specific.

2. Write down two action steps that will help you achieve your goal.

3. Identify potential obstacles to change and the strategies for working through them.

The following is an example of a development plan.

DEVELOPMENT GOAL

Let people finish their sentences before I respond. In other words, stop cutting them off when they are talking.

Action steps

1. Count to three after they finish their comments before responding.

2. Ask my colleagues to help me become more aware of the times I cut people off by providing me with feedback when I do—and don't—cut people off or finish their sentences.

Obstacles/Challenges	Strategies
Stress on the job—everything is a crisis and I just have to react.	Change my mindset. Think differently. Be conscious of how I make other people feel when I cut them off.
I'm used to behaving this way.	
At the time, I feel justified in interrupting, and only later realize it was not so important that it could not have waited.	Place a sticky note near my phone that reminds me to let people finish their sentences.
	Ask my partner to give me a sign when I cut people off.
	Make the effort to change. It will be awkward at first, but the outcome will be worthwhile.

DEVELOPMENT GOAL #1

Action steps

1.

2.

Obstacles/Challenges	Strategies

Notes:

DEVELOPMENT GOAL #2

Action steps

1.

2.

Obstacles/Challenges   **Strategies**

Notes:

DEVELOPMENT GOAL #3

Action steps

1.

2.

Obstacles/Challenges   **Strategies**

Notes:

DEVELOPMENT GOAL #4

Action steps

1.

2.

Obstacles/Challenges   Strategies

Notes:

DEVELOPMENT GOAL #5

Action steps

1.

2.

Obstacles/Challenges   Strategies

Notes:

DEVELOPMENT GOAL #6

Action steps

1.

2.

Obstacles/Challenges   **Strategies**

Notes:

DEVELOPMENT GOAL #7

Action steps

1.

2.

Obstacles/Challenges   **Strategies**

Notes:

DEVELOPMENT GOAL #8

Action steps

1.

2.

Obstacles/Challenges   Strategies

Notes:

ON-BOARDING CHECKLIST

When you start a new job, people will be expecting you to ask lots of questions. Take advantage of this period to learn as much as you can about the people, products, culture, roles, and procedures of your new situation. You will never have this opportunity again. This checklist is intended to help organize your exploration and guide you through the on-boarding phase.

If some of these items seem obvious, you have permission to roll your eyes. However, I would rather list five things you already considered if it means listing one that might not have occurred to you!

Come Prepared

❏ Review the Six Basic Connecting Needs and your Connecting Style.

❏ Enter having read and learned everything you can about your new department.

Your Attitude

❏ Enter as a student, humble and eager to learn and understand.

❑ Let people know that you are there to help in any way you can.

❑ Remember that as the "new kid on the block," you have to allow time for people to simply get comfortable with you. Expect some initial testing and wariness. Take it in stride as part of universal initiation rites, recognizing that this behavior is very temporary.

❑ Make an effort (even if you are shy) to meet as many people as you can—on your team and on your floor. Keep track of names, titles, and job responsibilities.

UNDERSTAND THE ORGANIZATION

This is your chance, before you dive narrow and deep, to learn in broad strokes what the organization you just joined is all about. Go for it!

❑ What is the history of the organization?

❑ What is the mission of the organization?

❑ What is the vision of the organization?

❑ What is the physical layout of the facility (plant, building)?

❑ What is the nature of the industry of which your organization is a part?

❑ Where is the organization positioned in its industry?

❑ What are the organization's products and/or services?

❑ Who are the key players in the organization (CEO, department heads, your boss, your boss's boss)?

❑ How are products manufactured or services delivered? Prepare a workflow.

❑ Who are the customers? How does the organization differentiate its products to keep customers happy?

❑ Who are the competitors? How do your products/services compare to theirs?

❏ How do the various departments interact to achieve the organization's goals?

❏ What are the organization's key policies, procedures, and rules? Include HR policies, risk policies, and procedures.

❏ Understand what your company's values and expected employee behaviors are around diversity, community involvement, and corporate citizenship.

DEFINE YOUR ROLE WITHIN THE ORGANIZATION

Doubtless someone will be orienting you to the specifics of your job, but be sure to explore your full relationship with the organization.

❏ What is your job specifically, and how does your job impact others? Where are you positioned in the workflow?

❏ Who are the people on your team? From whom do you receive work/instructions? To whom do you give work/finished product? What are the quality standards by which your work is measured?

❏ Who are the people to whom you may ask questions?

❏ What insurance and educational benefits are available to employees?

❏ How do sick leave and vacation leave accrue, and when are you eligible to receive/use them? How is time off scheduled, and how far in advance?

❏ What are your boss's expectations of you?

❏ What role will he/she play (e.g., mentor, customer, resource provider)?

❏ How does he/she prefer to be communicated with, and what is his/her Connecting Style?

TOOLS

It sounds simple, but most of us completely underutilize the tools we have available. Now is your time to learn to use them to their fullest.

❏ Practice using the tools of your trade, including e-mail, the relevant software, and the phone system. Put a mental filter on before you send an e-mail—your work e-mails should not sound like personal e-mails.

❏ Practice accessing the various forms or tools you will be required to use (time sheets, vacation planners, procedural documents, etc.).

❏ Adopt a daily organizing system and make daily organizing a habit, incorporating weekly planning and monthly benchmarks that tie into your annual objectives.

❏ Take time to navigate through the company website thoroughly. A wealth of information can be found there. Research articles about your company, explore human resources (HR) policies, read executive biographies, and look for training opportunities.

ACTIVITIES

The following are activities you may be able to arrange for yourself if they are not provided:

❏ Explore and sign up for any training or development activities that target new hires.

❏ Request a tour of the building/facility. Introduce yourself along the way. Include any departments with which you will be interacting. No tour? Explore on your own!

❏ Set up lunches with key people (your boss, co-workers, HR rep, etc.).

❏ Request relevant written information: organization charts, presentations, websites, policies, procedures, marketing brochures.

❏ Use your daily organizer, diary, or PDA and set aside time at the beginning and end of each workday to prioritize tasks, examine accomplishments, and plan your next steps. This is a good habit to establish and will help you succeed when the workload becomes heavy.

❏ Request a copy of personnel policies, risk policies, codes of conduct, and so on.

❏ Make note of fire and security procedures and exits.

❏ Interview people. Prepare a short set of relevant questions, such as "What does this person do?" and "How is his/her area related to mine?"

❏ Identify the top five to ten resources (websites, trade publications, associations, etc.) for learning information about your company, industry, market, product, customer, and so on.

❏ Ask for or find a mentor. Using a mentor can help you accelerate your learning, expand your network, develop your skills and behaviors, and enhance your career.

ENDNOTES

1. Barbara Kovac, "The Derailment of Fast Track Managers," *Organizational Dynamics* (New Brunswick, NJ: Rutgers University, 1986).

2. Elizabeth W. Dunn, Daniel T. Gilbert, and Timothy D. Wilson, "If Money Doesn't Make You Happy Then You Probably Aren't Spending It Right," *Journal of Consumer Psychology* (in press).

3. David W. Merrill and Roger H. Reid, *Personal Styles and Effective Performance* (Boca Raton, FL: CRC Press, 1991).

4. Adam Bryant, "He Wants Subjects, Verbs and Objects," *New York Times* (April 25, 2009), p. BU2, accessed February 20, 2012, at www.nytimes .com/2009/04/26/business/26corner.html.

5. Adam Bryant, "An Interview Is More Than a Social Call," *New York Times* (December 12, 2010), p. BU2, accessed February 20, 2012, at www.nytimes .com/2010/12/12/business/12corner.html.

6. John Wooden, Academy of Achievement interview (February 27, 1996), accessed February 20, 2012, at www.achievement.org/autodoc/printmember/ woo0int-1.

7. Charlie Rose December 7, 2009 www.youtube.com/watch?v=jtjDYXqt Ccg.

8. Jacob Weisberg, "Only Connect! How Obama's Cool, Detached Temperament Is Hurting Him and His Party" (January 23, 2010), accessed February 16, 2012, at www.slate.com/articles/news_and_politics/the_big_idea/2010/ 01/only_connect.html.

9. Maureen Dowd, "Visceral Has Its Value," *New York Times* (November 22, 2009), p. WK11, accessed February 20, 2012, at www.nytimes.com/2009/11/22/opinion/22dowd.html.

10. Kristi Keck, "Charge to Obama: 'Go Off!'" CNN (June 3, 2010), accessed February 16, 2012, at www.cnn.com/2010/POLITICS/06/02/obama.oil.spill.tone/index.html.

11. Samuel A. Culbert, *Mind-Set Management: The Heart of Leadership* (New York: Oxford University Press, 1996).

12. Michael Abrashoff, *It's Your Ship: Management Techniques from the Best Damn Ship in the Navy* (New York: Warner Books, 2002), p. 43.

13. Walter Issacson, *Benjamin Franklin: An American Life* (New York: Simon and Schuster 2003) pp. 56–57

14. Ibid., p. 57.

15. Ibid., p. 56.

16. Jonah Lehrer, "DON'T! The Secret of Self-Control," *The New Yorker* (May 18, 2009), accessed February 16, 2012, at www.newyorker.com/reporting/2009/05/18/090518fa_fact_lehrer.

17. Thomas L. Friedman, *The World Is Flat: A Brief History of the Twenty First Century* (New York: Picador, 2005)

18. *Taking the Leap: Freeing Ourselves From Old Habits and Fears,* Pema Chodron, edited by Sandy Boucher, 2010, Shambala Press]

19. Greg Mortenson and David Oliver Relin, *Three Cups of Tea: One Man's Mission to Promote Peace . . . One School at a Time* (New York: Viking Penguin, 2006), p. 79.

20. "Paul Allen: Office Politics, Behind the Scenes at the Start of Microsoft" (excerpted from the text), *The Economist* (April 28, 2011), accessed February 16, 2012, at www.economist.com/node/18617898.

21. Ernst & Young, "Groundbreakers: Using the Strength of Women to Rebuild the World Economy (2009), accessed February 16, 2012, at www.ey.com/GL/en/Issues/Driving-growth/Groundbreakers—Executive-Summary.

22. Ibid.

23. William Safire, "The Way We Live Now: 8-8-04: On Language; Groupthink," *New York Times* (August 8, 2004), accessed February 16, 2012, at www.nytimes.com/2004/08/08/magazine/the-way-we-live-now-8-8-04-on-language-groupthink.html?pagewanted=all&src=pm.

24. James Oberg, "7 Myths About the *Challenger* Shuttle Disaster" (January 27, 2006, updated January 25, 2011), accessed February 16, 2012, at www .msnbc.msn.com/id/11031097/ns/technology_and_science-space/t/ myths-about-challenger-shuttle-disaster.

25. Paul Krugman, "How Did Economists Get It So Wrong?" *New York Times* (September 2, 2009, in print September 6, 2009), p. MM36, accessed February 16, 2012, at www.nytimes.com/2009/09/06/magazine/06Economic-t.html ?pagewanted=all.

26. Ibid.

27. Ibid.

28. Ibid.

29. C. Kamau and D. Harorimana, "Does Knowledge Sharing and Withholding of Information in Organizational Committees Affect Quality of Group Decision Making?" Proceedings of the 9th European Conference on Knowledge Management (Reading, UK: Academic Publishing, 2008), pp. 341–348. Also based on I. L. Janis, and L. Mann, *Decision Making: A Psychological Analysis of Conflict, Choice, and Commitment* (New York: Free Press, 1977).

30. Shaun Rein, "How to Deal with Corruption in China," *Forbes* (October 7, 2009), accessed February 16, 2012, at www.forbes.com/2009/10/07/ china-corruption-bribes-leadership-managing-rein.html.

31. Josephson Institute Center for Youth Ethics, "The Ethics of American Youth: A Report Card on Students' Values, Attitudes, and Behavior (2008), accessed February 16, 2012, at charactercounts.org/programs/reportcard.

32. David Crary, December 1, 2008, (www.washingtonpost.com).

33. PriceWaterhouseCoopers, "The Global Economic Crime Survey: Economic Crime in a Downturn" (November 2009), www.pwc.com/gx/en/ economic-crime-survey, accessed February 16, 2012, at www.pwc.com/gx/ en/economic-crime-survey/assets/global-economic-crime-survey-2009 .pdf.

34. "Corporate Crime Is on the Rise: The Rot Spreads," *The Economist* (November 19, 2009), accessed (from the print edition) February 16, 2012, at www.economist.com/node/14931615.

35. Stanley Milgram, "The Perils of Obedience," *Harper's Magazine* (December 1973), pp. 62–77, accessed February 16, 2012, at harpers.org/archive/ 1973/12/0021874.

ABOUT THE AUTHOR

Over the past thirty years Steven Lurie, Ph.D., has emerged as a leading expert in the psychology of leadership development and organizational effectiveness. Through his coaching, workshops, and teaching, Dr. Lurie has helped provide thousands of individuals, from college students to industry leaders, with the self-awareness and relationship tools essential to succeed in the real world of personalities, politics, and pressure.

His books, *Connect for Success: The Ultimate Guide to Workplace Relationships* (2009) and *Handbook for Early Career Success* (2010)—have already been incorporated into training programs at KPMG, Prudential Financial, NYU Stern, University of Vermont, L'Oreal, JPMorgan Chase, UBS, BET Networks, and NYSE-Euronext.

Dr. Lurie founded the leadership development firm Lurie Executive Development in 1986, which specializes in coaching, team building, and collaborative change management.

He recently started *Empowered Life Strategies* to provide workshops and training for others who historically have not had access to the development opportunities normally afforded those in the management ranks of the private sector.

Dr. Lurie is currently Associate Clinical Professor at Adelphi University, Garden City, New York. He earned a B.A. in psychology from Brandeis University in 1975, and a Ph.D. in psychology from Adelphi University, where he then completed a four-year post-doctoral program in psychoanalysis and psychotherapy.

Dr. Lurie is a member of the American Psychological Association and NACE. Visit him at steve@stevenluriephd.com.

Made in the USA
Charleston, SC
04 April 2014